The Solitary Sentinel and Selected Poems. Copyright © 2019 Sonia Lowis. Produced and printed by Stillwater River Publications. All rights reserved. Written and produced in the United States of America. This book may not be reproduced or sold in any form without the expressed, written permission of the author and publisher.

Visit our website at www.StillwaterPress.com for more information.

First Stillwater River Publications Edition

ISBN-10: 1-950-33906-8
ISBN-13: 978-1-950339-06-8

1 2 3 4 5 6 7 8 9 10

Written by Sonia Lowis
Cover Design by Kristin Lombardi
Published by Stillwater River Publications, Pawtucket, RI, USA.

The views and opinions expressed in this book are solely those of the author and do not necessarily reflect the views and opinions of the publisher.

Nature & Nurture

Nature and Nurture

1. My Moonlit Garden 1
2. The View from Cap Juluca on Anguilla 2
3. South Wind Cottage 5
4. My Rock Garden in Spring 6
5. The Judge's Abode 8
6. Hidden Pastures in New Hampshire 11
7. Foam on Sand 12
8. Sand Dune in Snow 15
9. The Nordic Inn in Alpine 16
10. Touisset in Autumn 19
11. Beach Blessings Abound 20
12. The Deck House 23
13. Fall Evening on the Beach 24
14. Rachmaninov's Piano Concerto No. 2 27
15. The End of the Summer Season 28
16. Leaving 31
17. Winter Solstice 32
18. Frenchman's Creek in Florida 35
19. January 36
20. February Morning 39
21. Summer Perfect 40

My Moonlit Garden

Moonlight lends mystery
to my everyday world
its chiseled brilliance
carves shadows in
unexpected places
flower beds soft
as pillows
invite rapture
I revel in my childlike gift
to suspend thought
while staring in wonder
at the ho-hum familiar
transformed now into
black and silver
no birds sing
no traffic passes
somewhere a clock
strikes four
I'm blessed by this moment
enchanted by the vision
of everything old
become new again
new-born reborn
illumined by God's
divine touch
whose gentle radiance
floods my soul
and cradles me
in peace profound
and promises eternal

The View from Cap Juluca on Anguilla

Absolute tranquility
A crescent of powdered sand
Rims an azure sea
At my feet a gown is flung
Fit for a wedding
Scalloped lace smooth
Over cream satin
May I walk on water
Or is that just an illusion
The storms of hurt
And betrayal are past
I've navigated to safe harbor
And shrugged off regrets
With my winter cloak
I'm at peace suspended in time
Weightless translucent
Insubstantial as foam
But buoyed up with hope
For the future
Between my lashes
Butterfly-wing colors swirl
Aquamarine deepening to emerald
All shimmering with sequins
Where the hot sun strikes
Across the gulf
Streaks of purple meld
Beneath ageless mountains
Brooding below
Their benediction of clouds
I hasten my steps
Where the sporting surf
Carves chasms on the coral point
And a wave leaps
To toss a bridal wreath
High overhead
Showering drops of diamonds
On my expectant face

South Wind Cottage

A tranquil retreat hidden behind banks of cascading
multi-colored fragrant flowers and stately trees
located within sound of the ocean's surf
and clear sight of the circular koi pond...
A beacon of contentment
beaming forth bright light within and without...
What bliss to drowse on the blue-stone terrace
relishing the birch grove's dappled sunlight
and hearing the bees hum
as they feast on the blue agapanthus lilies
that flank the front door
or saunter to the elliptical emerald lawn beyond...
perhaps idle time away on the graveled north terrace
filling your senses with the musical
miniature waterfall
frothing over intricate mosaics of stone
where scarlet and golden fish dart in play...
The pool's surface reflecting rare willows
silent drooping sentinels whose tri colored leaves
shade the inviting pristine white bench...
Delicate decorative water lilies
suffuse the pond's surface with varied rosy hues...
Within the simple stucco structure
a wash of lavender below accents
lovingly acquired and much admired works of art
whereas upstairs harmonious pink
and a hand stitched quilt
among numerous needle pointed pillows
inevitably invokes smiles...
On warm summer nights the fluctuating tide
murmurs its accompaniment to drowsy dreams
before song birds sweetly herald the new dawn...
But now the advancing dusk
Of an approaching autumn evening
induces only a lazy lethargy leaving me
replete and at peace
and forever thankful to dwell
amidst such all-encompassing serenity...

My Rock Garden in Spring

*Grey boulders boundary my world like large-flanked elephants
sunk in ponderous contemplation at some water hole
turning their solid posteriors on lesser mortals
I smile when so many invited to view my flowers
exclaim 'but where did you find the rocks!'
where do rocks grow hurled down from quaking mountains
or heaved up from red hot depths
most likely slow tumbled at the edge of a glacier abandoned eons ago
when vast ice plateaus melted and the seas swelled close
today beyond the rocks scrub trees lift stark arms
in seeming supplication to a cerulean sky
providing perches for songbirds who herald each dawn
in melodic chorus with miniature timid peepers
hiding inside the rock's parameter where green things grow
myrtle and fascinating small succulents
cling to the vertical stone surface defying gravity
as crocus and hyacinth and golden daffodils
flourish in handfuls of soil sumptuously secreted in hollows
alas the vivid rainbow hued tulips
fell prey to four footed prowlers who've gobbled each bulb
and left behind wilted stems as guilty proof beside each precise hole
executed neat enough for a surgeon to envy
every day unfolds further wonders
magnolias and dogwoods reveal fragile blossoms
and soon a dappled canopy will leaf out overhead
when first azaleas then lilacs and lilies
will glow like varied vivid jewels
enticing the hummingbirds to come for solace
as they fill my heart with thanksgiving
and potent praise for the simple pleasure
of spring surviving yet another year
brimful with beauty and perfumed breezes
whilst proffering a healing balm
for each winter-weary spirit*

The Judge's Abode

Positioned at a perfect point
To embrace land and sea and sky
It's a painters dream
If they could capture on canvas
The serenity of slow-drifting clouds
Sailing high overhead
In the luminous sky
And reflected in limpid pools
Shielded by fringed marsh grass
Enabling the long legged wading birds
To forage in safety
In harmony with the wind's will
Sailboats bows ruffle
The sea's sequined surface...
To enhance our view
A center island appears to be arranged
Solely for best artistic effect
Away to the west
The Mount Hope Bridge
Is poised above the water
Suspended by silken threads
It focuses the eye
Returning a sense of reality
To this dream inspiring scene
Where ones spirits are lulled
Into a drowsy contentment
Praising our maker and nature
For creating
This life affirming paradise

Hidden Pastures in New Hampshire

Acres of sun-splashed meadows
to fragrant white hydrangea shrubs...
Warmth and color greet one within
where aromatic scents promise future delights
from the immaculate and well-equipped kitchen...
The massive drawing-room
is a treasure-trove of unique artifacts
which draws the eye and dazzles and enthralls...
The sweeping views from the terrace
over pastures pond and woods
to range upon range of misty blue mountains
hazy in the distance under heaven's wide arc
simply enchants...
A magical place where behind the solid stone structure
tucked into a corner of the woods
a genius has created a miniature chapel
simple in design yet profound in purpose...
How blessed we are to be welcomed to share
a glimpse of this earthly paradise...

Foam on Sand

How to describe it...
The tide is low the sand hard-packed
and scant ripples diffuse calm water
yet the wind is strong and its blown millions
countless millions of translucent iridescent bubbles
to cover this crescent of beach
they form a shimmering carpet under my feet...
I pause reluctant to trample a single fragile globe
but my aged dog harbors no such compunction
and lurches off stiff-legged in pursuit
of the myriad mass
which floats away from her advance...
Embarrassed by her brief skirmish
she shakes herself briskly and resumes
her habitual stance at my heels
steadfast in my shadow...
I carry a weight on my heart this day
and half frozen tears burn my cheeks
as words of Christmas carols
tumble unsung in my throat...
I mourn a son birthed on Christmas Eve
and assay once more to try and fathom
the feelings of Mary
as she awaits the birth of our Lord
the One who is to save us all...
Is the stark cross revealed to her
in the shadow behind
the brilliant blinding promise of His natal star?
We far outnumber these uncountable bubbles
each one unique and complete
fulfilling its too-brief purpose
to spread wonderment and joy
just as we each desire
to be born with boundless hope
unfettered and free to explore our own
unlimited horizons
as we learn to accept our human failings
and love and nurture the soul within us
beneath the benevolent gaze
of His all-perfect sight...
I breathe in the peace
of this picture-perfect place
yet ache with the knowledge
that in the west tinder dry grasses burn
consuming everything in a savage assault
whilst in the south unstoppable rain
has buried innocent thousands
in mounds of unholy mud tombs
why Lord why?

Sand Dunes in Snow

I stand before a canvass
where blue shadows slant
across a path of dimpled snow
edged by a few forlorn feckless
rose hips
dangling from wind-bleached plants
discolored and torn
the path rises toward the pale wash
of winter sky
mind-numbing in its immensity
silence complete
yet if I close my eyes
I can conjure up the dissonance of
laughing voices
and hear thumping bass radios
and visualize a restless parade
of self-conscious girls
posturing as they pass
groups of adolescent boys
who race each other
into the languid surf
while mothers gossip leaning close
in straining striped beach chairs
as babies sprawl on blankets
at their feet
grasping toward discarded shells
the vivid colors seem to ripen
and swell under the hot sun
now alas they are all long gone
only their ghostly echoes remain
caught in the skilled artist's
gifted brush-strokes
as the relentless wind
tramples brittle brown stalks
and the unending sea
folds in upon itself
in hypnotic repetition...

The Nordic Inn in Alpine

*Imagine... A dramatic drive below dense
fir-covered mountains creating a tense
twisting drive above the frothing waters
of the Snake River...
At last the vista widens to a valley floor serene
where sublime folks are found
soft-shoeing on the village green
as a mellow quartet evokes a nostalgic mood
the toe-tapping seniors come forth
fit to frolic and feeling good...
The evening clouds drift by backlit
dramatically by a lowering sun
while kids of all ages jump and twirl about
simply having fun...
Couples crowd under the silver disco ball
snuggling each other close
clearly still in thrall...
Hummingbirds flit through the sentinel pines
delighting a small boy
by alighting on his hands...
Strangers nod and smile enjoying the band
whilst comfortably seated we give them a hand...
Too soon its time to turn away and seek
our comfortable lodging and a good night's sleep...
We fade away to dream quiet dreams
throughout the tranquil night
each of us quite certain that tomorrow's dawn
will bring forth new delights...*

Touisset – In Autumn

A time warp world
where funky summer cottages
nestle snug between impressive new homes
all bunched together along the edge of the bay
seeking their heart's ease from the tides healing flow
a place where inherited friendships span generations
to stand steadfast against the erosion of time
while sun bordered flower beds spill bright blossoms
over the lush verge and tomatoes hang heavy on the vines
striped towels crowd sagging laundry lines
resembling miniature spinnakers
ballooning out on the wind's whim
tugging at their worn wooden pegs
above toppled sun-bleached canvass chairs
when evening shadows lengthen toward the cool of night
I yearn to freeze-frame the moment
reluctant to relinquish the sun's benign warmth
and these soon lost last lazy hours
for the too fast approaching frosty fore-shortened days of fall
I pause to absorb the scent of new mown grass
and drowse in the hum of myriad insects at my feet
under the high hedge a rabbit hunkers down
betrayed by a single twitch of an ear
I blink and its gone
overhead against the darkling sky a skein of geese fly south
their primordial cries drift down
like disembodied spirits seeking paradise
the nape of my neck prickles and I stand transfixed
staring across the wide bay
where golden windows capture the evening's closing light
and beam back a welcome from the further shore

Beach Blessings Bestowed

Above my head thirty-strong
a flight of geese murmur
their plaintive and primordial song
conjuring forth fragmented remembrances from
a time of ancient absolution
where I believe I once belonged
flying high in a perfect v
straight as a die they glide over me
before drifting soft
upon the slumbering sea
silhouetted by a pale sun
succumbing in the west
perhaps summoned forth
by my half-articulated request
to seek to comprehend our creator's behest
ere we each receive our rest
back-lit by ranks of serried clouds
the luminous light beams forth
a harmonious peace
above mere mortal's moderate reach
on this sanctified deserted beach
I lift my spirits to the unfathomable sky
from whence I sense
multiple benedictions flow
beyond the horizon's pearl-gray glow
joyfully anointing
our winter weary world below
measured footsteps pace
beside the measureless sea
invite meditation
to restore and renew me
I stroll this timeless
tide-strewn ground
humming hymns of praise
and hoping to accept
unbound blessings
as I breath the moist salt-tinged air
and linger to script
my destiny's dreams
in uncountable grains of sand
knowing each one to be hallowed
as they lie untrodden at my feet

The Deck House

The slanting evening light is trapped
In the lofty elms elegant grasp
Until a playful breeze
Releases handfuls of golden nuggets
Showering them down
Across the pale wooden deck
Tumbling brilliant patterns
Over bare boards
And stirring the brittle leaves
Discarded too soon
Into miniature cyclones
Where they rustle an invitation
To relive a child's delight
To stand knee deep in weightless heaps
Scooping armloads overhead
And laughing as they float down
In slow motion
Brushing bright cheeks and lips
And clinging to tousled hair
If only we might as easily retrieve
Our lost dreams
But its too late now
Too many world-weary arguments
Lost us our innocence
Too many melancholy days ago
Peepers cheep below us in the damp grass
As the sun sinks into the sea
And a tense time later when conversation
Again proves inadequate
I stand in the darkling gloom
As sighing waves strike the shale beach
With a melodic refrain
Soothing as a muffled heartbeat
From the time before
Conscious thought came
I drift asleep against your back
Weightless and dreamless too
lulled by the illusion
that I'm cherished in your arms

Fall Evening on the Beach

*I pace the empty beach
in serene solitude
whilst flocks of miniature
wading birds
take flight at my ambling
approach
then soon settle onto the sand
behind me
to resume their well-choreographed
ballet
dancing through the withdrawing 'waves'
foam-flecked retreat
to retrieve invisible sustenance
from the glistening sand
would that we were
so easily led
my shadow lengthens toward
the ever shortening
dusk
and as I turn for home
the western sky is set
ablaze
resembling a glowing cathedral
become brilliant
flood-lit
with stained-glass ambers
and vivid scarlets
paling to smudged purples
and pinks
as the sun drops
below the rocks
and the lapping waves pause
in mid-coil
to quieten and hush
listening toward the tall
marsh grass
where a harmonious cadence
of myriad peepers
commence their song
alas they foretell
the end of this too-brief
but still stunning season...*

Rachmaninoff Piano Concerto No. 2

Rachmaninoff in the morning stretches my mind
I limber my body to the background of beautiful intensity
that his noble music evokes his somber chords slow moving
toward resolution enable me to center myself
before I jump barefoot 20 imaginary skip-ropes
and then lunge in mock defense against mythical foes
I pause to refresh myself with sips of water and envision
a tauter taller toned-up me as my once sluggish pulses race
now to keep pace with the energy of his uplifting tempo
where did his genius spring from was he a loner tortured
by doubts who nightly prowled the corridors of his mind
in restless torment seeking inspiration
or did he sleep snug beside his soul's mate
if I read his biography would I understand his music more
or is it sufficient simply to revel in the sound
and open heart and mind to the promising possibilities
he allows me to glimpse within myself
so I grit my teeth and 'go for the burn' lowering my back
against the door frame's support before prostrating myself on
the pale carpet to begin leg lifts and the dreaded crunches
at last I sit Zen-like in an almost yoga trance
as the music pours over me like a waterfall
cascading liquid notes of perfection to submerge my senses
for sublime seconds surrounding me with glorious sound
until the final chord signals the end of my reverie
and releases me back to my ho-hum reality

The End of the Summer Season

The sun is still bright so I squint as I swing my arms
and stride along the low tide's object-strewn sand
seeking treasures from the sea and inhaling iodine
from the many heaps of discolored seaweed...
Gulls grumble at my approach
and hop stiff-legged a few yards away
before lifting into brief flight and settling behind me
on the hard-ribbed sand
the sea is almost motionless
reflecting glass-shards of brilliant light
and the pattern of clouds overhead
makes me smile in remembrance of the child
I once was who dreamed dreams
creating castles from fanciful shapes
and always eager to explore far away places
whenever a tall sail silhouetted
on the horizon beckoned...
I climb wind-weathered stairs
past rows of empty cabanas
and discover a discarded purple ribbon
tangled in a skein of seaweed
I pause to wonder...
Did the summer breeze tease it free
from a tow headed child's sun-bleached pony tail
or was it a decoration pinned to a daring décolletage
as violins shimmered melody under the striped tents
and couples swayed close together
beneath the moon's potent gaze
while the lazy waves murmured their approval...
Where is its owner now hunched over school books
as the summer's tan fades faint freckles from her face
or is some lithe long-limbed beauty
skipping cracks on city streets
and dreaming of ski chalets for Christmas...
I love this place and season best
when I am the sole beachcomber here
free to meditate or create fantasies
whilst the shorter days yet provide warmth
so I sprawl against a barred beach door
relishing the day and feeling blessed in the moment
and so grateful for so much in my life...

Leaving

Bent beige bulrushes on greige stalks
Frame the faint light filming a pale sky
my spirits lift with the expectation of days
void of stress and redolent of relaxation
and the tantalizing promise of romantic nights
when two become one captivated by the hope
that intimacy may create a bond of shared dreams
the elusive sunrise reveals nimbus clouds
dimpled like lambs wool against misty mauves
until pastel blues gain the ascendancy
stark trees stand sentinel like soldiers on parade
amongst last season's discarded leaves
strewn over gouges of red ocher earth
they exude a moldering moistness
their layers of decay dissipate slowly
in the sun's gentle warmth and probing light
an abandoned house reflects back flashes of purest gold
from cracked windows that bulge forward
pressed between paint peeling shutters
they hang askew on protruding nails
sunk deep into the spongy exterior
of rotten wood
the decrepit roof is pocked with decay
this winter will surely see its demise
the car's tires shrill their accompaniment
on the macadam's slick surface
to my buoyantly beating heart
as faster ever faster I flip the pages
of the slashed map in my lap
and smile while we hurtle on
toward the next bend in the road

Winter Solstice on the Shore

At close of day I yearn to explore
The ever-constant always changing
winter shore my key unlocks a yellow door
and on my in-born breath I see
vistas of luminous clouds almost to eternity
wind-gusted gulls sweep low their mewing cries
snatched away by the ebbing tides
whose storm-blown foam rims our coast
where ships may shatter on ancient rocks
those picturesque rough-hewn blocks
where fossils show sea-creatures swam
ere the ascent and fall of man
can our cosmos' clock be reset
does our primal dam
miss our unsteady steps
away from her consoling depths
is she aware of our exploitation
how long must she bear the humiliation
of civilization's mounds of refuse
and renew herself amidst our misuse
ever returning good for evil
hoping to spare us from supernal fear
whilst proffering us her boundless sphere
overhead bruised clouds take late flight
revealing shell-pink lambent light
sunset solitude plenitude peace
shadows slant low as waves lave clean
where ancient prints are no longer seen
must we follow that bygone band
or may we bring ourselves to hand
as freshening breeze ruffles surface calm
piercing our searching spirit's balm
and forcing us to face our mortality
we must accept that each day's gift
is balanced with a debt
in eon's past by nature herself was set
hat unborn generations still unmet
may find a welcome when they come
to this our fragile island home

Frenchman's Creek Florida

A place of natural beauty where creeks and ponds
provide playgrounds for the playful otter
And the slow-paced way of life
is perfectly suited to golf cart transportation
An idyllic retreat for the discerning
and deserving few
cosseted away from the often crazy
realities of life today
in the good old US of A
Vistas of manicured acres of golf greens
entice and delight the eye
while tennis and pickle ball engage the more energetic
There are also multiple unique exercise apparatuses
with experienced experts
to put you through your paces and keep you limber
Holidays bring families with their exuberant young
to splash in the pools
or stroll the beach and body surf the ocean swells
Perhaps to relish a moment of quiet contemplation
and appreciate the bounty of nature's beauty
or relax under a masseuses skilled hands
Service is always prompt and punctilious
accompanied by warm smiles of appreciation
In short this is a pristine paradise
Fully engaging all one's senses
with hope for the future that this special enclave
may long remain to inspire and welcome
the many generations yet to come

January

*A smear of snow dimples
the uneven ground
as a shrill hawk
slices through
The crisp air...
Silence envelops me
penetrating through
my frail defenses
to fend off the icy cold...
My brain and breath
both frozen
until I deeply inhale
the crystalline air
and shrug off my brief malaise...
Suddenly I'm hopeful
as each day's light lingers longer
responding to the warming sun...
My horizons must also broaden
to embrace the eternal spring...
That brings to each of us
its multiple promises
of new birth
and new
hope...*

February Morning

Sometimes its good to be alone
to welcome the gift of each new day
at my own unhurried pace
to be aware of the rhythm of my pulse
and relish mundane thoughts
I putter about in a wooly robe
shuffling along in fuzzy slippers
like some candidate for an old-age retreat
my orchid's buds have swollen with promise
during the long night
and I marvel now in the new light
at the intricate design
on my espaliered pear trees
highlighted against their brilliant white
crisscrossed support
its early still and the lawn lies hard frozen
patches of ice prevent any possibility
of ripples on the brackish pond beyond
save the merest wisp of sea-smoke
conjured forth by our Creator's hand
to lend majesty and mystery
to the tranquil scene
I feel secure in HIS love
and my heart hymns HIS praises
while a songbird alerted by the dawn
warbles a fluting melody
the sun's warmth dissolves the frost
into iridescent diamond designs
across the lengthy lawn
replicating the border of tall trees
I set down my mug of tea
Smiling and eager to transpose
intense emotions
into simple words

Summer Perfect

I sink onto my padded chaise
Shielding my eyes
from the bright light
as the sun's slanting rays
highlights explosions of vivid indigo
from the potted plants
beside the cottage door
a low stone wall
edges the pond
where lazy fish float
among sculpted water lilies
beneath the small waterfall
a sudden splash
draws my attention
to the granite bird bath
where a robin and a cat bird
vie for precedence
smiling I close my eyes
relishing the harmony of bird song
And the rhythmic pulse
of the not far-distant waves
embracing the hard packed sand
a miniature buzz alerts me
to the darting presence
of a hummingbird
among the dragon flies
this is my Eden
my fantasy borne fruit
as fish and fauna
share this small paradise
of perfumed lilies
and tiny rock-thriving plants
a car door slams
and an excited voice exclaims
"Granny it's me!"
And so I stand
to embrace the reality
Of my little life
come full circle...

Friendship

Friendship

1. An Ideal Relationship 47
2. Elm Street on the Point in Newport 48
3. The Onset Pointe Inn near Cape Cod 51
4. Curious 52
5. Tanglewood 55
6. The Conductor 56
7. Because I'm Me 59
8. Jo-Anne 61
9. Self-awareness 62
10. RTW 65
11. Barbara's Block Island Retreat 66
12. OM 69
13. Mary 70
14. Polly's World 73
15. Polly's Pool in Palm Beach 74
16. Pool Exercises 77
17. First Snow 78
18. Winter Ski Vacation 81
19. Seeking Winter Sun 82

An Ideal Relationship

Aware and responsive to our mood
generous with touch
a quick handclasp when you settle into a car
a warm hug when you pass in the kitchen
and the unmistakable look of welcome
when you enter a room...
Also simple words of love
"I thought of you today when...I saw or heard...
And wished you were with me to share the experience
what would you like to do tonight?
Tomorrow? This weekend?"
The gift of patience to listen as we struggle
to express emotions
and in the night a murmured endearment
or gentle caress
just to let you know they're glad you're there
and are aware of your feelings...
Also the bonus of humor
and the ability to find joy in small things
and possibilities in the midst of difficulties
with the generosity of spirit
to share and thereby lighten
potential problems...
That's all that anyone desires
kindness costs nothing but it pays dividends
every day of our lives
and brilliantly enhances
our hopes for all our tomorrows...

24 Elm Street on the Point in Newport

Green pitted pears
On blackened stalks
Dangle from the
Knarled old tree
Under a mottled
Evening sky
Traffic thrums
On congested streets
Nearby
But the manicured lawn
And harmonious
Flowers
Bestow a soothing balm
On my restless spirit
As I recline supine
On the white string
Hammock
Beneath a painted gourd
Stirred by an errant
breeze
I hum tonelessly
Under my breath
As the lengthening
Shadows
Allow the indulgence
Of an absence of
Thought
Appetizing scents
Waft from a window
And I'm content
To wait
Feeling cherished
And nurtured in this
special place
By the kindness
Of friends...

The Onset Pointe Inn Near Cape Cod

I awaken in pre-dawn light
and stroll to the balcony
and tuck my chilled feet into a chintz-covered
cushion on a white wicker chair
I stretch and inhale the pungent sea scents...
The world below is formless
an enigma of unsettled yet sensed motion creating
silhouettes and shadows...
Near shore drowsy seabirds murmur
as they drift on the tide's turn
and wisps of fog diffuse in the brightening light
then quietly vanish before my curious gaze
the earth smells new-made...
I treasure a tangible tantalizing hope
that we may yet create a secure future
imbued and invigorated with practical idealism
to rescue and restore our tired old world...
As first light streaks the sky
stars fade and a crescent of sea grass
becomes a smudged outline etched into the
dimpled sand created by a skillful hand...
I loll back and close my eyes
listening to the wind's importuning harmony
as the sailboat's rigging thrums
its accompaniment to an unfurling flag's
crisp staccato pulse
whilst anchored to earth it strains
ever skyward...
I meditate in mute homage
humbled by my mortality and profoundly moved
by this enduring and pristine seascape
as I dare to dream dreams...
Suddenly a restless songbird's single note
announces the end of this perfect night
proffering me the priceless gift
of an incandescent and dazzling new day...

Curious

*It seems that
it's my turn now
to ask if you're
OK?
Or even alive?
Or simply sadly
surviving?
Or maybe dead?
Or just staying
in bed?
Indulging a spark
for someone new?
Or possibly feeling
a trifle bit blue?
Perhaps you're
celebrating
some unexpected
success
with characteristic
excess?
Whatever path
you may
have chosen...
Please pause
For a moment
to consider
the untimely
forsaken
yet still loyal
old friend
from the road
not taken...
Who yet remains
steadfast
and is still
concerned
and even
a tiny bit caring
but most of all
just curious...*

Tanglewood in the Berkshires

*An oasis of
manicured
lawns
and tall
trimmed
trees
set in
extensive
grounds
rimmed
by lakes
and hills
a sacred
sanctuary
where
liquid notes
of melody
hang
suspended
in the
rarified
evening air
for the
rapture
of a
discerning
and
applauding
audience*

The Conductor

He strides upon the stage aware of the thousand eyes
that measure his purposeful step
murmurs spread at his approach
like ripples in a swift running stream
he is simply an ordinary man yet with baton in hand
he assumes the mantle of the immortals
and is transformed as he sculpts images out of air
commanding the diverse audience to exhale as one
our very heartbeats now are synchronized
to the music's pulse hypnotic evocative irresistible
he is our sole focus his arms assume the power
of an eagle's wings beating in measured flight
and sweeping us into a rarified air
that saturates all our senses
compelling us to free float and dream dreams
sometimes the music's force propels him off his feet
and we too are suspended in space
before he goads the strings and brass
like a picador poised to control their energy
and blend it seamlessly into a lyric harmony
in the next phrase he becomes matador
executing a delicate passage with admirable restraint
and calm assurance before assuming the role of lover
and wooing us into relinquishing our individuality
to embrace simple reverence and devotion
our separate selves sublimated now
into the universal ecstasy of shared sensation
the last note lingers fading into quiet
and we hold our breath in rapt attention
but all too soon applause erupts
ripping apart the silence
and splintering us back into our fragmented lives
as we stumble our separate ways home
toward our holy or unholy rest
but in that last coherent moment before sleep comes
we may be blessed by the echo of the magic
wrought by one man whose upraised arms
pointed our way all too briefly toward paradise

Because I'm Me

I wish to see
kindness
flowing
toward me
I need to feel
affection
in your
touch
and I want
to know
that you're
OK
as I pray
for
all our
tomorrows
embraced
by
nature
gentled
by
nurture
whilst
God's
promised
peace
enfolds
each of us...

Jo-Anne

When it all began
Could she possibly comprehend the doctors' dire
pronouncements?
That froze her brain and strangled her breath...
Bombarded by 'protocols'
Her horizon shrank to that day's 'meds'
Whilst beyond the stark sterile reality
Towered the loving support
Of her family and too-numerous-to-mention friends
Their concern gentled everything...
United in their determination
That this precious woman
Whose generous spirit means so much to so many
With her positive outlook and rare courage
Must surely beat the odds...
Days crawled past waiting for test results
Orchestrated by her doctors' expertise
Until inch by inch small miracles
Built upon a fragile base
And optimism banished dread...
We were awed by her patience – and acceptance-
When small things went awry
And her interest in each one of us
remained undiminished
Humbling and true...
And so she became for us
an example of all that is best in life
crowning victory over adversity
and never giving up and never giving in
And trying always to express the love
Which we carry within our hearts
That and so much more we learned from her...
Now her transformation is complete
And she steps forth
Like a brilliant butterfly
Spreading her luminous wings
to enfold each of us with her devotion
As we are all blessed to relish
the joy inherent
in this brand-new day...

Self-awareness

To love another demands self-worth
'Thy neighbor as Thyself'
the courage to trust your heart
requires sound mental health
faith in the future and inherent respect
encompassed by a realistic self-image
reflecting the mystical beauty of life
to give thus ennobles a thousand fold.

Rejection shrivels self-esteem
as a drought destroys a flower's fragrance
so abandonment becomes a dark journey
for the suffering soul
an unkind word
or careless gesture
can destroy trust
between forever friends.

For if not friendship to forge the way
how many mortals capture
the immortal harmony of love
and consummate the mystical union
which transcends all prior experience
bestowing a benediction beyond price
to revere and savor
and above all else to share.

RTW

He creates beauty
but is self-effacing.
Has strong opinions
"You know what I mean."
Yet may voice them shyly.
He's no stranger to pain
or disappointment
but may be relied upon utterly
and somehow still retains
an innocent optimism.
A man of conviction
and integrity.
He's a large but gentle presence.
Slow gaited swift witted
his words always
kind
with accents familiar.
His eyes alive with humor
he's vastly amused
by our confrere's
foibles.
But generous in judgment
and infinitely loving
with family and friends.
We talk lots
and laugh much.
We share our feelings
in total trust.
I bathe myself
in his regard
and feel secure
supported
and even serene
with a stirring sense
of optimism
for our shared future.
Emotions lap against me
like an irresistible
tide
drawing me toward total
fulfillment.

Barbara's Block Island Retreat

Part hermitage part cloister
and wholly a place of nurture...
By nature blessed with tranquil beauty
of vast vistas of sea and sky
a place of wind-swept sunlight and luminous sunsets
a mystical place of sacred stones and silences
enabling spiritual renewal...
A safe place to share past hurts
and illuminate a path toward a healthy future
beyond the merely physical...
A place to absorb the blessings
of meditation and yoga and prayer
with time to limber and fine-tune our bodies
even while we expand our minds...
Above all else a place to learn to trust again
supported by faith and each other
we strive to honor those promises we made
to seek out God's purpose for our
too often too frenzied lives...
So we sing 'Hallelujahs!' In joyous celebration
of our unique ability to create and cherish life
while we appreciate the diversity
of the God-given gifts we glimpse
within ourselves and one another...
We bestow and partake of absolution
for past regrets and failures
even as we hunger to share our vision
with other weary pilgrims who endure
the daily manifold burdens that life
casts across their path...
So we seek to pursue His eternal truth
and leave the island revitalized
with peace in our hearts
and a profound reverence for His radiance
flowing freely for us all
from His never-failing
and always constant love...

OM

Omnipotent omnipresent Omega
from the time before time
ceaseless unchanging all-embracing
transforming cleansing fulfilling
focus on a single breath
create a brilliant internal light
in a world oft gone dark
expand your soul's awareness
in the lonely void
trust enough to free-fall
into nothingness
and risk everything
to encounter the supreme
ALL
disconnect mind and limbs
and allow the unknowable
entry
dare to lose yourself
in that quiet small space
and be gathered close
to the eternal heartbeat of
OM...

Mary

She embodies love
Love of family close friends
And life itself
She knew better than most
how tenuous and treasured
each day is and she embraced
them full measure not just the easy
comfortable polite surface of things
but the dark and painful
and confusing aspects as well
she epitomized valiant acceptance
of whatever came
fragile fine-boned refined
exquisitely dressed always
she could dominate a room with her
marvelous voice and gift of laughter
quick intelligence
not above puncturing the posturing
of fools
with her sense of the absurd
few could take offense
whatever cruel challenges life threw at her
her indomitable spirit enabled her to
rise above the hurts and fears
to focus instead on what
made her heart sing
her family and closest friends
and their concerns hopes and dreams
loyal and discreet she was blessed with
common sense and gave shrewd advice
nobody's fool she knew how the real
world worked and she could use
her knowledge to advantage
she didn't flinch from hard facts
but she did not allow them to destroy her
she possessed the extraordinary gift
of acceptance
she could live in the moment
inspiring all of us
to draw strength from her example
of what is essential
to truly live life abundantly and well
and we're blessed to have know
and cherished her...

Polly's Pool in Palm Beach

Incomparable setting...
The last rays of the dying sun
turns the lake to liquid sheets of silver
under a multi-hued molten sky
brushed with palest pink strokes
shot through with flame
as it fades to smudged mauve
yet still has strength
to tip each miniature wave
frothed forth by my lazy feet
into purest gold...
I lie nerveless and relaxed
in the tranquil tropical warmth
and feel waves of love
flow from the house
lapping over me as the ripples
extend to the end
of the pool...
I am blessed by my friendships here
in this special place of sanctuary
where winter-weary souls
find illuminating inspiration
that lead us to seek
a deeper purpose for our lives...
Beneath the surface
of this polished pristine place
our life's journey flows forth
from its humble beginnings
to embrace multiple blessings
here on earth...

Polly's World

Blue and gold scintillating like sapphires and diamonds
at first glance a glittering and beautiful image
shielding the empathetic warmth within...
At still of night a train's haunting cry
echoes across water
amplifying childhood's jumbled remembrances
and bittersweet dreams...
Nearer dawn the wind chimes commence their melodic song
stirred by an errant breeze
fragrant with the scent of gardenias
soon the sun arcs overhead into a cloudless azure sky
to warm the temperate turquoise pool below...
Exotic plants edge a sinuous curve of lawn
As it stretches toward the shimmering lake
where endless progressions of pelicans
play follow-the-leader above the dancing waters
as though choreographed by a comic
all too soon the ubiquitous 'phone
commences to ring... and the day begins...
Aerobics in the pool or sprints on clay courts
precede a shower and quick change for lunch
perhaps an elegant charity affair or buffet at the beach
maybe just a sandwich seated beside the golf links
wherever she's seen hands and smiles reach out...
So many are aware of her unique mix of knowledge
can-do efficiency and old fashioned 'goodness'
(for who among us has not felt better for confiding in her)
her expert advice is sought on a wide spectrum of subjects
and she juggles the pressures of too many commitments
better than most...
Mid-afternoon a restorative tea tempts toward over indulgence
yet provides a moment of calm while nostalgic piano tunes
induce a rare reverie and hypnotic waves
sweep toward the embrace of picture perfect palms
swaying to the music as they fan the light air
whilst amazing yachts drift by on the gulf stream hugging the horizon...
Too soon there are more messages to retrieve
and another quick change before attending an art opening
or book signing - theatre - concert - musical - ice show or ballet
perhaps even a simple dinner with friends...
Cosseted by luxury secure at the center of a widening circle
of family – close friends – animal causes - and multiple kind deeds
she strives to balance all the clamorous claims
with deeply felt personal needs
And another day in the fast lane in this earthly paradise
flows into peace while she sleeps...
I pray her every wish may be granted
By HIM who has divine purpose for every searching soul
And holds us fast in the security of HIS perfect love.

Pool Exercises

When Dan the man comes to Polly's pool
we have to follow the golden rule...
Be kind to one another and yet, look sharp!
His hard rubber balls may sink you like a shark!
His corny jokes help keep us afloat
as we labor and sweat treading water like pros!
as we struggle perforce...
'Neath secret high hedges on chic Lagomar
to capture life's essence
not hide it in a jar...
No! No!! No!!!
We exert our bronzed bodies
stretch and polish our minds
in fine comradery
whilst shimmying our behinds!
It's a simple known fact that
life's abundantly good
when Dan uses his charm
to soothe and to calm
sometimes
troubled waters...
And with consummate skill
as we each do his drill
he's able to refill
our occasionally sinking
psyches...
So we labor and laugh
then relax and rebound
eager to explore our always new-found
and even profound...
Curiosity
Over what comes next?

First Snow

A profound stillness an abeyance of sound
and a total absence of color
as the view from my window
proffers an other-worldly vision
of beautifully diffused light
illuminating soft round contours
glimpsed between spiraling swift-building mounds
of winter's wild wind-tossed snow
it gentles all sharp edges
of entangled tree limbs
whilst cocooning me in tranquil isolation...
Sudden surprising snatches of birdsong
followed by a flash of scarlet cardinal enchants
in this almost silent almost white dream-world
ethereal and entrancing it encapsulates
memories for me of shared childhood adventures
I catch my breath and snuggle beneath quilts
hopeful to pursue peaceful reflections of the past
until the reality of your recent message ravages me
and the vast distances between us
with you on a beach in Malindi
increase my feeling of helplessness
and intrudes upon my interior dialogue
to intensify my concern for you...
Aware now that you face grave health issues
I am led to pray for all of us inherently flawed mortals
who soon may suffer the ultimate loss of self
yet as we commence our final journey
toward the consummate mystery
I must believe that we do not travel alone
but that our every faltering step
is shared by HIM who draws us toward
the beckoning perfection of HIMSELF
in whom we place our loving trust
I pray you know that you are loved
and will be very much missed
and so my dear
and always adventurous sister
travel forth in faith and peace...

Winter Ski Vacation

Snow scant
yet ice clogs
streams glimpsed
under the shade
of dark pines
the road rises
voices shrill
tensions taut
as bated breath
obscures
car windows
spirits sizzle
as greater height
displays depth
of snow
expectations
and tales tall
views charm
snacks fill
and suddenly
snow's assured
explosion
of activity
doors slam
poles jam
faces freeze
fingers numb
pulses leap
mountain and hearts
high
air's cold sun's bright
snow's white
in seconds
I'm in flight
bliss!

Seeking Winter Sun

*Gloria's
on car radio
inspire
confidence
wet road
sodden fog
cold air
cannot
dampen
anticipation
of joy
for this
transformative
Christmas Eve
dusk
and the
approaching
holy day
appears
at dawn
as we seek
the southern
sun
love
within me
devotion
surrounds
goals set
should be
met
in the
new year
ahead
where
blessings
surely
abound*

Angst

Angst

1. In Memoriam for a Lost Love 87
2. Rainfall 88
3. The Daisy Chain 91
4. Torn 92
5. Dawn 95
6. See-Saw 96
7. Bittersweet 97
8. A Weather Change 98
9. Dark Day's Journey Nowhere 101
10. A Moment in Time 102
11. Valentine's Day 103
12. Torment 104
13. The Path Not Chosen 107
14. Alone and Alive 108
15. A Glimpse of Paradise Lost 109
16. Rivals 110
17. Waiting for the Return of Love Lost 111
18. Endings 112
19. Passion Sunday 113
20. False Hope or Hope Realized 114
21. Frustration 115
22. A Drear December Dawn 116
23. Dispirited 117
24. Christmas Eve Tragedy 118
25. Storm Warnings 121
26. Today 122
27. A Scrap of Soap 123
28. A Year has Passed 124

In Memoriam for a Lost Love

You pervade my existence
invisible skeins webbed
beneath my skin
bind and monitor my heart's pulse
you still enhance my vision
twin my thoughts double my delights
as you ameliorate my sorrows
and soothe my soul
do you dwell in my dreams
as obsession
remembered love yearned for lust
or perhaps only an echo
from a half-forgotten
used-to-be pretend life
why still such power
to cast a net so wide
that you entrap
my future peace
and engulf my emotions
futile to flee
your scents sounds textures
tantalize memory
languid fingertips lavish
indelible softness
to tease liquid lips apart
whom would I be
without thee
ever hurting always lonely
merely mortal me

Rainfall

*Rain on the roof rouses me from sleep
drumming demanding incessant insistent
I long to be clasped against your warmth
and delay today's dour dawn
but I lie alone always alone
and the rain mocks me taunts and torments me
that winter is near and my defenses thread bare
I have no reserves of joy
nor pink cheeked glow or a heart gladdened
with the easy remembrance of love shared
the relentless rain tip taps splattering my window
seeking entry signaling dwindling days
and deadening hope
salt tears splash into a rising tide of emotion
churning with failed possibilities
I strive for calm and conjure up a dream
of some tranquil retreat
where I might drift in a watery embrace
learning to accept the limitations
of my life
as my yearning spirit
ascends through leaden clouds to seek
the buoyant brilliance beyond...*

The Daisy Chain

He loves me he loves me not
she wants me she wants me not
casual couplings
transitory pleasures
as you watch your own performance
with inflated ego and fragile psyche
do you falter
or strive to obliterate the face
mere inches from your own
and replace it with the haunting
succubus who robs your sleep
or that other once-innocent one
who would have lain down
her life for you
does your body remember mine
and miss it
or will any available body do
you're getting older
and perchance maturing
emotionally
one might as well chide a child
for his greedy grasp
wanting everything
for himself
careless of the other's feelings
all surface not substance
as long as we act 'nice'
do you really believe
we can ignore past pain
and avoid a mangled future
did you ever know
how it feels not to be alone
to give yourself so completely
that in that selfless act
you are blessed
with total fulfillment?

Torn

I'm
broken
torn
apart
tugged
in half
told to
go here
then
told to
go there
when
or where
to benefit
whom
and for
whose
welfare
I know not
I know not
I'm unable
to care
anymore
anyway
any time
any day
or anywhere
why

Dawn

The song bird is mute ensnared in a cage
beating fragile wings against confining bars
what tinsel glitter lured the poor finch
from its gentle pursuits 'midst hedgerow
fields and glen
was it a whim of fate or the curse
of an over-optimistic imagination
coupled with the blithe assumption
that there exists a universal
code of decency amongst men
to nurture and cherish
their captives
alas she has forfeited her flight
and now waits in peril
see how the delicate wings tear
and the bruised breast
spills scarlet drops
impaled on spite
her dreams wither
and her eyes flutter closed
whilst her wounded wings fold
across her faltering heart
yet still she struggles
to keep faith
with a dimly felt hymn
reverberating deep within
a tiny sliver of hope promising
penance suffered
and atonement paid
so when a new day dawns
perchance a gentle hand
may reach between the bars
and release her
into the fresh air of freedom...

See-Saw

I am a see-saw up-down up-down
one moment a hero
the next moment a clown...
Up-down up-down queasy and dizzy
all the way round...
Try to reach for a star
and you bump to the ground...
Dare to dream dreams as you stand in the dirt
try to smile nice whilst inside you hurt...
Up-down up-down the proffered prize
just out of reach
it's one of life's hardest lessons to teach...
Pride and patience may wither ere long
everything blurs and nothing belongs...
You offer your heart
but 'tis your mind they steal...
Faster and faster scalding tears fall
choking your throat
life's naught but a joke...
Up-down up-down to crash or to fly
up toward the ever beckoning sky...
Sickened and saddened
you sag to the ground
as the dance defiantly whirls on by...
Songs soon hush and the music ends
but you're broken and bandaged
with nothing to gain
just hoping 'gainst hope
that none know your pain...

Bitter Sweet

Love, at first, was just a game to us
Mock-serious we laid down boundaries
forbade depth or substance
set a too-brief time allowance for our play
I like to think you grew in stature
to meet the onrush of my passion.
That first startled, you were later as proud as I
Of our perfect, effortless union.
There were postponements
interruptions to our harmonious game
but now the umpire has called it done.
Score sheets swept clean by salt tears,
tattered by the scything wind.
But the victor must grant
a prideful withdrawal to the vanquished
and so I stumble to say 'good-bye'
as my words falter, fumble, and fail
where actions once flew true and swift
winging to you from my overflowing heart.
Forgive my self-indulgence.
Accept sincerely my warm thanks
for the value that your love has brought
to a forgotten life.
For the hope that all we learned together
may yet benefit those others whom life decrees
that we should partner,
Enough! I loved you to the furthest corner of my soul.
And love you still. I always will.
And so I keep for you my promise to us both:
To leave you to your life.
Immeasurably enriched I hope,
as I, by the remembrance of a bliss
whose promise was not ours to keep.
Go happily my love.
Know always that your words were true
When you wrote:
'Both are losers in our game...
Yet share one sweet sorrow for from our parting
one hope renewed.
A love uncompromised by corporal union
Can still unite our souls...
The game well won
victory ahead! And shared.'

A Weather Change

Wind moans below the eaves
haunting as a lost child
icy tendrils creep 'neath doors
pierce knife sharp in my heart
drab hours rob ambition
opaque dust drifts stirred by drafts
time crawls in mute supplication
vacant stare evade
as furnace rumbles and bills mount
the future's fearful and funds are low
no endless night for my tormented soul
just punishing progression
of uncertainty
cold the ground lies hard frozen
bleak boughs frame gray skies
cruel wind frets the fabric
of my thin cloak
beneath the surface spring waits
marshaling forces marking time
in a moment or a month on a whim
or in response to prayer
nature's harmony swells the buds
give praise
undying undiminished
the invisible gift is given
our earth embraces the age-old rite
glory revealed
new life new season new hope
reborn transformed
awaken my soul
to a gentling breeze
under an innocent azure sky
and accept a kiss of benediction
from the sun
while lambs frolic
and bright-eyed robins
and earnest bees explore
the miracle of creation
among a carpet of flowers

Dark Day's Journey Nowhere

Unshed tears lacerate my throat
unfocused eyes gaze blank
unnumbered nights and
dawnless days drudge by
my world's confines
shrunk
to the parameters of my bed
where I must alas
occasionally rise
and force myself forth
in the well-rehearsed role
of attentive guest
or obliging host
whist wondering within
does anyone else
ever endure
this same repetitive
and tedious routine
of marking time
waiting for nothing
as hope ebbs away
and day after dragging day
passes by
I am as a discarded leaf
fallen
upon a stagnant stream
drifting in senseless spirals
in dizzying
slow motion to nowhere
for no purpose
pray God not like this
always and forever...

A Moment in Time

I once was carefree in a cozy cocoon
my days dawdled games of bridge dulled
but duty prevailed and there were compensations
a large family endearing animals good friends
and nice neighbors
all tidy and neat and rather bleak
whilst deep inside I marked time wondering
if some inspiration should seek and find and fulfill me
and then out of nowhere suddenly you were there
thunderclaps of passion hammered my senses
lightening bolts of electricity prickled my skin
your tenderness stabbed deep inside exquisite pain
I fell into your arms seeking your soul
my defenses gone I tumbled out brand new
how did fate find and unite us
a gentle man understanding and caring
compelling and yet oddly unaware
I was uplifted stretching to reach new heights
to capture and hold fast your interest
my increasing desire
to fill your world with self confidence
and complete you wholly
I promised us all sensual pleasure
and unrestrained joy
in an endless shared circle of bliss
but alas we inhabit a cynical world
with laws we cannot change
and guilt twin to sorrow
for our former obligations
dragged us down
casting a cloud over our golden days
so there was no escape
save to return to prior claim
wondering wordlessly if worn-out duty
should supplant certain rapture
now a cold curtain of despair wraps around me
stifling fevered thoughts whilst assuring grief
inside my resumed routine I feel robotic
living on automatic pilot heartsick
and powerless to respond

Valentine's Day
(An Emotional Massacre)

*Its lonely when no one
remembers
it hurts when there's no one
to care
its sad when there's nothing
to plan
and worse when there's
no one to share
its hard to envision
the future
if no one is waiting there...
What became of our
memories
discarded like yesterday's
news...
Why change the dial
on the radio
to hear only repetitive
blues...
When did too much become
not enough
will you never learn
the lesson well
that you cannot expect
from someone else
emotions they cannot
reveal...
So move ahead
and don't look back
if he scarce noticed
your presence
he'll survive the
lack...
And so my former lover
God speed
and fare thee well
let there be only
peace between us
instead of this
eviscerating
hell...*

Torment

I scream in the silence but no one hears
my hands clench my face contorts
and the incurious world passes by
I taunt myself relentlessly
deliberately set times for stabbing inquisition
moments alone in bed when I drag out
each remembered image recalling emotions shared
are they still real
in the pathetically dwindling hope of only one
to partake of life fully and become whole
you must first know yourself
and then be completed and complimented by another
secure from this base you can face
all life's challenges with courage
but ah when you are once again alone
agony blocks your every breath
pain pools behind your eyes
food nauseates and sleep denies
and you are merciless on yourself
you little fool you dared believe
that you could find and share a paradise
denied to ordinary men
and where others kept a sense of perspective
and self-preservation
you gave totally and emptied yourself
no one can see into the mind of another
by nature's decree we often deceive
and most usually ourselves
yours the tragedy for just once
to recognize truth - blindingly -
but now it's gone the bubble burst
no longer languid days
to exalt and explore passion
but slow-motion minutes of torture
to drag through alone
you face the phone that never rings
and fool when it does you tremble to answer
and always it is no one from nowhere
as your mind blanks and your hands fumble
the room spins and you force your voice
past the agony of disappointment within
learn from this little one
duty writes the rules - not love

The Path Not Chosen

You were my source of joy
invigorating challenging
and always fulfilling
I believed we must love each other forever
I perceived you as a giant of a man
feeling privileged I brought treasures to share
the tragedy lay in your myopic view
of yourself...
A lack of nurture in infancy
or misperceived inadequacy in adolescence
perhaps scarred by poor choices in maturity
impossible now to assign blame
for who is wise enough to heal old hurts
and rebuild shredded self-esteem ? Not I
I 'd given all of myself unstintingly
and emptied myself to my innermost core...
We were well-matched I thought
we shared similar views friends hobbies
and I hoped our hearts
in the secret silence of the night
we created a unique intimacy
profound and beautiful
beyond anything previously
dreamed...
Should I have guessed that you
felt constrained by my love
overwhelmed and even guilty
that you could not always respond
satisfactorily?
Each subtle evasion on your part
pierced dagger sharp
slashing away my self esteem...
I struggle now seeking
surcease from the unrelenting
burden of pain that weighs me down
as I try to surmount the abyss
that swallowed all my simple pleasures
leaving behind a hapless hole
in place of tender hope as I attempt to face
the unremitting loss of you from my life...

Alone and Alive

We lived life on different levels
Although for a too-brief time
we connected on concentric
overlapping circles
that closed out the madding world
and gifted us with the illusion
that we were complete...
Brooding now brings naught but pain
breeding bitter regrets worn thin
by hapless helpless memory
that forces the captive mind to twist and turn
through a minefield of evocative events
edited into disintegrating fragments...
A heart may empty itself
pulsing pumping and even bloodletting
as it beats its tattered quadrants against burnt-out
remembrances
and emotion strangles in inflexible cobwebs
that crisscross the hapless psyche...
I renounce the struggle now and strive to breathe free
seeking no more this cynical mate
but instead one equipped with the rare gift
of an unsullied soul
willing to share a true essence of spirit
behind the fragile façade of face
and strive to create a solid foundation of truth
beyond the mere mouthing of words...
Love and passion and desire
cannot survive frozen under glass
as dried up emotions
eviscerated dissected and then discarded...
By God's decree and nature's realm
love must float free
playful loving nurturing and eternally optimistic
but tethered to reality by mutual trust
and a commitment that's wedded to respect
and bound up in a profound sense
of shared responsibility
alas... This time... It was not to be...

A Glimpse of Paradise Lost

How not to awaken in the dreamy night
and hug myself in rapturous memory of you.
How not to feel beautiful or wise
or capable of giving infinite pleasure.
Not hear music: strident trumpets, subtle guitars
or to sing with the dawn chorus of birds
and see the colors of the rainbow
immeasurably enhanced by my new insight
into creation.
Not to know present, practical, piercing truths.
Not to feel that I belong in God's world.
To seek insanity and so escape – peace
To dial the phone beside my pillow
And hear your voice – ecstasy!
To leave the country
And embrace the warmth of old friends
What cowardice!
To try and fathom your future – what futility!
I pray that she deserves you and knows it?
That together you may love again.
When I am no longer blinded by the dream
I dared to dream
Survival dictates that I should seek again
The completion of sharing my soul.
Or are we allotted only one love
In one life time?
Is it possible that you pretended
Surely had you felt as I
you could never walk away
never leave me to be so alone.
Cynics say that infatuation dies a'borning
and we'd have years to repent our madness
or instead perhaps create a warmth the world would envy?
Pain stabs through my protective forgetfulness
as images of a rock by a reservoir, a deserted beach,
and rosy blinds drawn over sun-filled windows,
as thumping music passes us by in the distance.
clench my heart and blur my vision
Do you too remember?
How it felt not to be alone any more?

Rivals

Alas I cannot make you
love me
your practiced touch
ignites my still surface
to molten fire
liquid with desire
I want you

You suppress a groan
plunging a knife
hurtful in my heart
are you thinking of her
must I share you
with a ghost

I would prefer
a more equal contest
surely none could love
you better
none more eager
to soothe and satisfy

I wish to fill your life
with an abundance
of joy but I cannot
foretell all
only you can choose
and will you?

Waiting for the Return of Love Lost

I feel dismembered
like a marionette toy
discarded on a dusty shelf
lift me down draw me erect
I may suffice for the moment's whim
or perhaps I'll amuse
for the duration
of the affair

Is a woman's place
secure in a man's heart
or are we only ornaments
to wear on his arm
consider well and best beware
there lies staunch strength
beneath my playful exterior
and smiling facade

Deep within there beats a
loyal heart
tempered by patience
while keeping rhythm
measuring out courage
but able to accept pain
ever tolerant and always hopeful
for the future

Women have much wisdom
to share
and offer a unique view of life
whilst embracing expectations of love
oh foolish man
who might settle for a mere
comely exterior and miss
the essential essence of life

Endings

I am no stranger to pain
he is a respected implacable
adversary
but I am ill prepared
for his stabbing assault
that robs my breath
and freezes my brain
alas I have no defense
against the numbing lethargy
which disrupts my sense of time
as I read and reread a single line
absorbing nothing
customary routines evaporate
familiar sleep denied
and a void despoils my soul
will I survive the future
my well-loved landscape
is obliterated
the abundant cup sucked dry
discolored pictures in damaged focus
drift through my mind
my body feels disconnected
magnified are slights and evasions
all the petty misunderstandings
which stalk a relationship
and shadow the loving embrace
in the light
alone how may I assuage grief
how heal the wound of his absence
how not remember the intensity of
bodies merging
the revelation of completion
when first confronted
by the 'other-self'
recognition half yearned and prayed for
then fully realized
how rare in this short life
to ever feel not-alone

Passion Sunday with Ungrateful Offspring

A time of conflicting truths
and heart stopping contrasts
jubilant crowds sing Hosannas
and on the next breath
brutishly howl crucify! Crucify!
So too do some who kneel
in public devotion today
destroy all semblance
of compassion and tolerance
within their private lives
when the cheerful bearer of gifts
is met by twin frozen statues
whose plastic stance focuses
overhead on the far wall
freezing the warmth from a
smiling face and forbidding entry
as they seek to deflect past memories
through the tortured prism
of their biased imagination
puffed up with false pride
they essay to rewrite the past
and shrug off all honest burdens of regret
honor they father and mother
and brothers
is a truism which one day
may return to haunt them
as envy and malice
take root in their cold hearts
where inward-looking lives
seek a superficial perfection
whilst closing out our Savior's bounty
that is poured forth
in an abundant stream of healing balm
to anoint all who possess
the gift to forgive
nourishing each flawed
but wholly human soul
on their steadfast pilgrimage
toward the ultimate cross
of conscience...

False Hope or Hope Realized

Inflated once my dreams flew high
like a child's balloons
reaching for the sky
circumstances beyond my control
shriveled each one
devoid of color they collapsed
where a cruel fate
crushed them to oblivion
I feel insubstantial
deprived of direction
where may I turn
to seek resilience
and like a bough bend
not break
when forces threaten
but strive always
for inspiration
to explore new heights
I must heed the whisper
of my conscience
and learn to nurture
roots of reliability
even as I put forth
tendrils of trust
as eager blossoms shine
through unexpected
drifts of brine
wishing to receive
the gift of new birth
just as sap rises each spring
from the sacred mystery
deep within
to swell each small bud
with a promised purpose
of completion
whence comes the courage
to accept the incarnate gift
and relish life's expectations
believing they are destined
to be achieved

Frustration

*Clouds press
low
and wind
tortures
the brow
of the hill
in the hollow
at my back
all is still
so still
shadows tease
me
I strain to see
the prospect's
drear
and the future's
obscure
save for my
need
of Thee
will I still
be here
when the
clouds shift
and will you
be waiting
when the fog
lifts
shall I know
myself
in that further
time
when the sea
retreats
and the land's
at peace
and then
are you mine?*

A Drear December Dawn

I dreamed of you again and lay still
to prolong the perception
of your arm snug across my shoulder
secure against your chest
the fragrance of your breath
warming my cheek
as you drifted into sleep
nuzzling my lips
our legs linked
our hands fluttered a caress
we breathed in unison
at peace in the embrace
of a compassionate universe
was it magic
that brought us together
how do souls find and fuse
in the midst of this
careening careless world
tragic to discard the gift
and dull of heart to seek
to replicate the mystery
in mere casual coupling
and be burdened by regrets
or risk annihilating loneliness
am I my brother's keeper
as we travel separate paths
do we search still
for commensurate fulfillment
that has seemingly slipped away
among the many sad lessons
from the broken past
or may we be given the chance
to allow our spirits to soar free
again and seek the bliss
we once so effortlessly shared
that is my dearest wish
my hymn of hope
may you be well and know
that I miss you still
and always will

Dispirited

Was I ever once that young
Free of foreboding
an ebullient optimist
Unbowed by hard lessons
Unscarred even by injustice
I rejoiced in my independence
And sought to discern His will
As I danced with springy step
Through the Eden of my imagination
Praising God for His good gift of life
Relishing nature's harmony
And often moved to tears
by the genius of music
And other people's words
Fearless of the future
I trusted in His love
Now all around me
I sense desolation
An abeyance of trust
an absence of joy
In some friend's lives
Where burdened by regret
they falter in spirit
As fear grips their minds
and freezes their hearts
Evaporating hope
One must be blind not to see
Deaf dumb and deadened
to divinity not to respond
So I creep forward
with stumbling gait
And grope with clumsy grasp
to seek His purpose
For our poor shriveled lives
as my prayers dwindle
Become arid unanswered unvoiced
expectations shrink
They're few and fragile
and easily frayed
By a careless glance
or unkind gesture
They fret my mind
Still I struggle for patience
and yearn to trust
His promise that
He will be with us
Until the end of time

Christmas Eve Tragedy

A yearly torment to so vividly remember
and be compelled to relive the painful past
as anguish assails me
obscuring the peaceful present
to reveal stark images
that stand out amidst the devastated rubble
of the long-ago...
Then the much-anticipated birth of a son
on such a holy night brought joy
yet from the first I felt a fearful premonition...
Today those well-worn memories
collide coalesce and torment me still
for that perfect tiny body concealed
great damage birthed within...
How now to ever forget those urgent night-flights
to Boston's hospital
with a frantic unsafe drunk driver
where the doctors' poker faces haunt me still...
I existed moment to dragging moment
on the knife edge of hope
in a wasteland of emotional isolation
whilst seeking to suppress the mounting
certainty of disaster
and somehow preserve my other sons sunny faces
as I assayed to survive the immensity of his loss...
Today my pain is exacerbated
by the self-seeking cruelty of one surviving son
grown into a facile superficial adult
whose words wound
and for whom I feel little now save pity and shame...
And so I turn away from such empty hostility
to show a brave face to caring friends
and share with them
in the manifold possibilities
inherent in today's multiple gifts
whilst feeling truly blessed by my other son's
devotion and understanding...

Storm Warnings

The sullen sky burdened by clouds
Envelops tattered tree tops
Bending their fragile tips
Much as an old crone's
Stooped back
Hunches under the weight
Of a shabby coat
An icy wind shreds
The crust of clouds
Forcing them to smother
This universe
In a dense murk
Suffocating and obliterating
All sentinel objects
Temperatures plummet
The very cosmos
Appears lifeless and stilled
Piteous creatures pause
Seeming even
To hold their breath
Agonizing in vain
If bolts of lightening
Could destroy all
In a consuming blaze
Or might there be found
Some mitigating force
A providential power
That could dissipate
This mordant state
And initiate hope
By sending shafts
Of celestial light
To pierce the gloom
And find a way
To heal and illuminate
A loving
and sustaining entity
Patient yet empowered
By faith
To believe in the promise
Of a peaceful and bountiful
Blessed new day…

Today

Raindrops smear tears
outside the car window
trickling vertical lines
in the dust
smudged like days old
mascara under weary eyes
traffic threatens on all sides
while oppressive thoughts
plod on
with leaden weight
burdening my soul
anxiety has sucked
all color from my world
the new year lies ahead
tenuous resolutions
sabotaged
by yesterday's regrets
that unbound
the demons of doubt
pricking my conscience
and dissolving
desire
I yearn for quiet time
while my unhinged mind
tumbles about unbidden
unresisting
as questions evade answers
"In God's good time"
is my mantra my motto
a lifeline stretched taut
from today's disappointment
toward the promise
of an eventual eternity
and please God!
Peace at the last

A Scrap of Soap

The rock garden towers taller than the house
An ice-age remnant of a moraine
I struggle to confront the days' arduous task
To cut back too-many dead lily stalks...
I miss him fiercely
How we laughed together recently
Sharing good memories when he lugged away
the detritus of dead daffodils
To help me...
A white elliptical lump catches my eye
Placed carefully in the center of the cold coiled hose
At the remote corner of the house
It is sticky and unpleasant
Crisscrossed with coarse hair
The reality of his present situation
Knocks me to my knees...
In this hidden corner of the garden
He must have bathed and shaved
And then slunk like an animal
In the shadows of shrubs to cross the lawn
And sleep in the shed
Until I called the police to oust him...
This bright son once excelled at sports
And his vivid imagination rocked a room with
Unfettered laughter
He was canny at finance and his advice revered
Until he was felled by a mental imbalance
Now I fear him...
I exist minute to minute on the knife-edge
Of high alert ever-attuned
To his unpredictable mood swings
And unreasonable expectations
And ever-escalating demands
that no one could fulfill
They choke my throat and sear my senses
Is my sole choice
To place him in God's hands?

A Year Has Passed

Has he remembered the silver cup?
How futile to relive it all and still to obsess...
This gift of his was a symbol he said
of our eternal involvement
a belief that once joined in passion
nothing could ever separate us...
Yet fate forced me away
and he could not stop me...
As the seasons pass
and the year dies again
I accept one thing: that I was mad to return
to the loveless confines of duty
to hurt a little more at each day's neglect
and to find myself buried
under a slag heap of regrets.
Agony to engage in speculation.
Does she care for him as I did?
Are our young unaware and untroubled?
Are casual friends enough?
Why must I continue to honor
a promise made when our love was new
that always, always I would be there for him
waiting and willing and helping
through the best and the worst of it...
Now I grasp at filaments of faith
imaging one day a very old man
with knarled fingers and wheezing breath
finding a tarnished cup
in some forgotten corner.
As he traces its perfect symmetry
will he pause to explore a small dent
and might a long-buried memory
stir to life within him
illuminating the pledges that we made...
That I was his definition of love
and he in turn was magic for me.
I seek now to restore a balance to my life
to find some purpose to this steep path
that I trudge along alone.
And yet I believe beyond all reason
that he still holds in his hands
all the inner secrets of my heart...

Love & Passion

Love and Passion

1. Autumn Sunrise 129
2. First Light Insight 130
3. Perfect Repose 131
4. Away in Wyoming 133
5. My Love 137
6. Last Night 138
7. Birthday Eve 139
8. Do you Believe in Magic 140
9. Skibo Castle in Scotland 142
10. Night Secrets 144
11. Anchored on Serena 147
12. Desert Dawn and Dusk in Arizona 148
13. A Starless November Night 151
14. A Summer's Day 152
15. If I Could Turn Back the Hands of Time 155
16. Maui 157
17. A Dream Voyage 158
18. Memories… 159

Autumn Sunrise

You've gone
and there is smoke on the fields
soft as a caress
it gentles an embrace across the land
"Do you know why it's there?" You ask
I nod smiling
you recite a quick explanation
and I relish watching you
accepting that you already know
everything
I will ever want to learn
but my explanation is simpler
mist drifting from hayfields
on an autumn morning
is pure magic
a visual enchantment to enhance
the mystery
of my love for you
it diffuses slowly
in the sweet morning light
perhaps tonight it will form again
and perhaps tonight you'll lie
with me again
then I believe I'll awaken
to the promise
of endless bliss

First Light Insight

I awaken from sleep
shaken by the remnants
of disquieting dreams
and seek to dislodge
the disturbing shards
in the security of your arms
at your touch a kaleidoscope
of colors ignites
dissolving slowly in delight
transforming tranquility
into blazing hot desire
as urgent needs are met
incoherent murmurs
speak the universal
language of love
in timeless time beyond time
we fall back sated
as prisms of brilliant pigment
dance behind our eyes
painting vistas of unimagined
beauty unfolding surrounding us
I cannot stop smiling
our transcendent coupling
complete
vibrant lilacs scent our dim room
and the cooing dove's dawn song
is a melodic chorus
seeming to applaud
our purpose here
as two separate selves unite
sanctified by the ultimate act
of creation
a harmonious whole humming
a joyous refrain
revealing to us
the sacred purpose of life
whilst thrusting us on toward
the promise of our
immortality

Perfect Repose

I sleep cushioned in comfort
cocooned by love
nestled against your back
I breathe as you breathe
lying beside your skin
inside your heart
languid sleep drifts us apart
thighs touch but dream-weighted
response is slow
you awaken first to male glory
and prod my side
insistent searching promising
I sigh and shiver as skin quickens
but drowsy dreams linger
you nuzzle my neck
lips touch tongues tease
and I want you
hands explore velvet textures
excitement trickles in my groin
face you restless and importuning
urgent in my need
your voice is gruff your hands are gentle
I am where I wish to be
you press your advantage
and I accommodate you
slave to your desire and giddy with ardor
seeking a rapturous release
you fill and fulfill me expanding my horizons
as you nourish my soul
you speak I cannot   I can only feel
as lust is transformed by love
a miracle as old as time itself
and still as young as our hearts
newborn and joyful
in discovering
each other

Away... In Wyoming

You dominate my thoughts
and enhance all my hopes and expectations for tomorrow
each night I drift into sleep imagining myself
securely nestled against your chest
while your exhaled breath warm as a caress
puckering my quickening skin...
Then the night air teases the curtain into lethargic motion
above my solitary bed and I shiver and turn
reaching out for you...
Musing of you I leave my bed to wander aimlessly
and wonder wistfully
if you too lie awake restless and missing me...
Venus and Jupiter share my lonely vigil
until dawn dissolves their savage brilliance
diminishing them to mere ghostly glimmers
glimpsed amongst the shadowy outline
of the stalwart pine which frames
my log cabin window when I seek brief relief in sleep...
Too soon the sun commences her preordained climb
to take command of the day
my summer hours are long but seldom self-indulgent or lazy
I trudge the uneven ground aware of altitude
in this land of pungent sage and high-pasture...
The unearthly cries of peacocks or hawks
against the thrumming intensity
of the ever-present Wind River
are a constant accompaniment to my reveries of you...
Your steps hastening home
to sweep me into your arms in welcome
when your lips and fingers entice me to an afternoon of languid loving..
Or your hands pliant on the steering wheel
until you turn to me
with a well-remembered well-loved intensity
in your clear blue eyes and your hands clasp mine
then linger longer to stroke my thigh...
Alas my mundane duties pass the time
until the night comes when I am at long last alone
and dare to dream dreams and remember how it was
and yearn to be reunited with my bliss...

My Love

Hazy with happiness
I lie back and gaze into bright blue eyes
intent upon my own...
You smile at me
and I shiver with anticipation
but your smile is gentle your mouth is soft
and your hand is deft...
I shiver again under your fingers
and each touch ignites a molten jolt
beneath my silken skin...
They delight and distract me
wherever you probe and caress
I need no mirror image
to excite
you steal away my will
flooding my breath and brain
with hot desire
so I crave only a total connection
to you
only you always you...
All else superfluous
yet each surrender
feed's my soul's yearning
and deepens my dependence...
What to do?
What to do?
What to do?

Last Night

We broke bread
And poured wine
Symbol of joy
To celebrate
The sanctity
Of life
And love
We kiss murmur
endearments
And sleep entwined
Bodies bump soft
in the night
Hands clasp
While whispers
mute
Nurturing nourishing
naked
And with the dawn
Subtle strokes
Alert each
heartbeat
To savor
Immortality
Separate senses
merge
Ignite and blaze
All consuming
Not to be
denied
We relish and indulge
Each caress
Enticing exhilarating
erotic
Explosions of color
Suspend coherent
thought
Lavish laughter
without limits
An epiphany of peace
An eternity of
love

Birthday Eve

You are my hero cerebral athletic and fun
My heart skips when I see you
I yearn for the caress in your voice
You've taught me so much
Igniting my body to surrender
And freeing my brain to race my computer
I never ever thought you were like
Anybody else.

Because of you other men bore me
Their subtle overtures appall
Only you understand and offer completion
Together we chuckle at the innuendos
Behind the headlines
Please don't let us become just like
Everybody else.

Where does love go its hard to sublimate passion
If we squander or dilute it with somebody else
Why do we seem compelled to focus on all
The distractions that threaten to overwhelm us
Can't we filter life through the prism of our love
Surely we are worth fighting for
Because we're not at all like
Anybody else.

You are my muse the music singing
In my soul my island of trust and tranquility
'midst the struggle of a rare bad day
I trust your judgments and share your ideals
As I love to lean against your strength
We feel empathy for lonely friends searching
For the gift we've found and perhaps wishing
We were just like everybody else.

But you and I are magic
Incredible harmony draws us close
Dissolving separate selves into a shared supreme
Kindred spirits and best friends
I love you much and want you still I always will
Let's defy the gods and beat the odds
Challenging the world to see the truth about us
That we don't need anybody else.

Do You Believe In Magic

Have you ever
 languidly
  roused
 From a dream-weighed
  slumber
   on a frosty morn
 and found a
  unicorn
 prancing upon
  your lawn?
Where ice-sheathed
 spears of grass
  flash
   blinding-bright
   in the
   dawn's
   new light...
The mythical
 beast
 bows low
  inviting me
  to mount
   so I tangle
 my hands
 in his silken
  mane
   as he transports me
   to a deserted
 beach
 where we laugh
 and sport
 far from
the gentle
waves' reach
 I close my eyes
  against the wind's
   rush
   and awaken
   in bed with an
   Adonis
   and blush...
 Mysterious, compelling,
  addictive
   and virile
 was ever a girl
  so blessed
 by the surreal...

Skibo Castle in Scotland
(Or perhaps Brigadoon)

Once in every hundred years...
Or if truly blessed once in a lifetime
reality blends into rapture
illuminating a paradise of possibilities
impossible to capture or predict
and elusive as smoke...
It yet creates an indelible image
back lit for a fleeting flash
of unanticipated delight
bewildering to evoke
in this usually predictable
pedantic and even prosaic part of life
where this provocative new element
has taken center stage
a grand illusion and a priceless gift...
My heart sings and my spirits soar
as I amble along an overgrown
Scottish carriage drive...
Bird song accompanies me
sun and shade caress my face
as I savor the invigorating air...
I pause to marvel over my perception of you
your humor voice demeanor and best of all
your actions and reactions toward me...
The loch gleams silver through a filigree of ferns
and sheep graze under woolly white clouds
in pristine pastures beneath unfettered acres
of heathered moor...
I skip over a puddle souvenir of last night's
quenching shower
and barely resist the urge to hug myself
in remembrance of your compelling touch...
On that thought cool hands fly to flushed cheeks
and my laughter floats behind me
as I pursue the playful breeze
quixotic and giddy and intent
on exploring all these myriad
and tantalizing new talents...

Night Secrets

*Cool sheets warm hands
and a rising sense
of rare excitement
suffusing my limbs
as distant water
burbles its musical theme
beneath the castle's
crenellated tower
I feel as any princess
might
captured by rapture
and capitulating
as I lie pliant
in your arms
hazy with happiness
my being fully
absorbed
into the fantasy
that at the pulsating heart
of this unique existence
is you only you always
you
caring and cherishing
and pleasuring me
you define an indefinable
promise
of fulfillment
your deft touch
ignites an urgent need
stroking deep within
my secret
self
sensitive skin shivers
in ardent anticipation
and on my indrawn breath
all reality recedes
and I am aware of nothing
save you...*

Anchored On Serena

The blood red orb rises
from its bed of ocean green
in minute increments
the sole movement on a mirrored sea...
I hold my breath in awe
of the approaching dawn
too soon the sky is transfused
with apricot and tangerine
transforming the Great Salt Pond
into swirling streaks of luminous pastels
lapping the boat's sides
and reflecting back clear light...
I am held captive
by poignant memories
and recently expired dreams
recalling past summer sails
when first light was lovingly shared...
Classical music
from some hidden source soothes
but a foreign comb displayed
beside a speckled mirror
evokes stabbing speculation...
I tossed restless in a half-sleep
last night
searching for the lost comfort of you
I strive to meditate
and bow my head in abeyance
toward the rising sun...
It freely bestows its brilliance
arcing high overhead in
slow motion glory...
I trail my hand through
the limpid water waiting for the launch...
I am renewed in this pleasing place
optimistic and eager to explore more
as we putter off joyfully accepting
the incandescent gift
inherent in this perfect sun-splashed day...

Desert Dawn and Dusk in Arizona

Today is touched by magic
slow-wakened from swift night's
best-dreamed bliss
Fans in secret recess
stir languid light
we speak soft and move slow
lying entwined
we wave intrusive time away
and watch it hurry by
secure our loving promises
shall stay
forever and forever
and a day...

The cool of early evening
brings a benign balm
and eerie brilliance
to erase the distorted view
of the heat-shimmering terrain
and flood the undulating miles of sage
with penetrating roseate light
illuminating ancient faces
hidden among the volcanic pipes
and crags of long-exploded craters
fitting burial vaults for long-gone gods
where long-lost rivers
once greened their fertile courses here
now long-since dissolved to dust
and guarded by naught now
save spare sentinel saguaros
a Bach fugue resonates from car radio
creating perfect harmony
for this treeless timeless territory
where pure desert air and gentle sound
assemble to dissolve all past regrets
and bequeath instead
the benevolence of serenity
beneath heaven's high arc

A Starless November Night

I dreamed of you last night
and awoke smiling
and lay still to prolong the perception
of your arm across my shoulder
held secure against your chest
the fragrance of your breath
warming my cheek
as you drifted into sleep
nuzzling my lips
and kissing me soft
our legs were linked
our hands fluttered caresses
as we breathed in unison
at peace in the embrace
of a caring universe
was it magic
that brought us together
how do souls fuse
in the midst of this
weary world
tragic to discard the gift
and dull of soul to seek
to replicate the mystery
in casual coupling
or be burdened by regret
and annihilated by loneliness
am I my brother's keeper
as we travel our separate paths
or do we search still
for commensurate fulfillment
maybe life's hard lessons
will be learned and somehow
set our spirits free
to seek effortlessly
all that we once shared
that is my noble wish
as I lie frozen and alone
on this frigid night
may you be well
I miss you still
and fear I always will

A Summer's Day

You are to me the breathless promise
of a summer sunrise
slowly the sweet warmth
dispels the night's vapors
and my anticipation for
this day dawns brand new
how sure I am of you
how confident that in all
you give to others
the essence of yourself is
distilled for me
we've traveled different paths
yet the parallels astound
our appetites well matched
shining confidence
lighter than air
expands my heart with joy
blessing me with a new
perspective
so I may absorb the beauty
you create for me
enchantment contained in each
fragile leaf
dancing in dappled shade
as passing clouds sail
overhead and beckon us toward
the glory of fulfillment
in a sunlit pasture
laughter stilled
we turn to each other
and pause to savor
a tangle of honeysuckle
distilling sweet fragrance
into the drowsy air
humming with bees
as swallows swoop low
our eyes meet
and the surroundings
dissolve
we're aware of nothing
save our need
to complete each other

If I Could Turn Back the Hands of Time...

Safe warm and fulfilled
you showed me secrets within myself
that I had never known...
In giving myself so completely to you
I was able to receive you more...
We were greedy wanton infants
cherishing each new experience
made more precious by sharing...
We were certain that life
would return to us full measure
all those favors so richly given...
Each new day dawned luminous
as a perfect pearl shines its radiance
upon the slender ribbon of time...
We did not care to hoard the idle hour
after surviving suffering
we innocently believed that now
life would right out wrongs...
We seemed fashioned for each other
every breath every glance thrilled...
Laughter and love consumed us
I felt boneless as a cat under your caress...
Until lust stole my breath
and my need was great...
Always you understood and restored me
perfect love so generously given...
Nothing held back
we were fearless in sharing all
our many moods past regrets
and every intimacy...
So much beauty to be discovered still
there were no boundaries between us...
We understood that there would always be
more passion to explore
more gifts to share and laughter to learn
How naïve we were
To think the world well lost
Harsh reality too soon intruded...
To hold us fast in frozen oblivion
Where we feel nothing...

Maui

An achingly pretty place...
Sea breezes sway tall palms and bird song greets
the dawn as exotic fragrances perfume the
languid air and plashing fountains frame
distant misty mountains...
Pure perfection...
"Only one ingredient missing..."
As a long-gone lover once wrote to me
from his similar sun-splashed island...
For shared love alone truly possesses
the effortless ability to seduce the senses
and guild the merely ordinary
into a rare treasure that may afford us
even a glimpse of eternity...
Allowing us precognition of our immortality
a flash of insight that may not be held fast
but demands to be free
to alight and illuminate at will...
Ah! How to secure the wisdom
to accept and savor 'the cup half full'
and still the lonely heart and
lighten its burden of unshed tears
as it mourns the absence of the
self-renewing abundance of mutual love
that joyfully and generously given
must nurture those so blessed
in an overflowing plenitude of peace...
Better by far to root one's dreams in reality
and forego impracticality
settling instead for simple friendship
a rare enough jewel in today's
supercritical super-commercial crass
and ever impatient brave new world...

A 'Dream' Voyage

Soft music lulls as the prow presses on
whilst the turbulent wake churns away
all past regrets and fevered stress
and mere mundane cares...
Let's set the clocks back
so day by blissful day we'll idle time away
and in this precious time out of time
we'll drown away care
and lovingly learn to share
all that is best within ourselves...
We'll slide through the hours
as we splash in the salt pool
or saunter to the sauna
or glide into an embrace
enchanted by the melody
swaying us close whilst the music plays
and the floor tilts under our fleet feet
so many choices so little time...
So much to explore
and you to adore
as a new horizon beckons
and a new life begs to be lived...

Memories...

Last night in sleep you came to me
softly you said my name and called me love
my shallow hurting self
deepened in response
and I was flooded through
by the possibilities
in your insistent words
sparks of hope rekindled anticipation
drawing me back to the warmth of life
from a frozen limbo
your love has made me whole
opening me to undreamed of possibilities
that promise so much
how may I find the words to thank you
how ever show you what you are to me
for you I wish myself lovely and wise
the forlorn nights of wasted years
now banished forever
I've come alive and will thrive
believing the world will soon see
the joy we yearn to share
it's a simple yet profound truth
to be fulfilled in the embrace of another
bestows profound happiness
surely our purpose here
to share our innate humanity
I will try to never fail you
to never casually accept the gift of you
but always seek to appreciate
the unique fate
that brought you to me
to be my friend my lover and my life

Seeking New Worlds

Seeking

1. The Solitary Sentinel Near Tennessee 165
2. Alaska 166
3. Stour Head, England 169
4. Birds in a Gilded Cage 170
5. Lake Windermere 171
6. Still Life in Beatrix Potter's World 172
7. Plockton on the West Coast of Scotland 173
8. The Isle of Skye 174
9. Avebury 175
10. Cruising to Nantucket 176
11. The Bitterroot Ranch, Wyoming 179
12. Benbecular House, Turks and Caicos 183
13. Escape to Block Island 185
14. On the Brink Leaving NYC 186
15. Island Paradise in the Dry Tortugas 189
16. The Low Country 190
17. Cruising the Beagle Channel, SA 193
18. Venice 194
19. The Village Gabriella, Tuscany 194
20. Sunday Morning in Oregon 197
21. Islesboro, Maine 198
22. Norwegian Dream 200

The Solitary Sentinel Near Tennessee

Traffic streams chromium gleams radio's blare
and brakes shrill as we speed by directional's blink
and few think of the mighty oak glimpsed amidst
the road's race I'm arrested by its stark grace
traffic converges careless of consequence
in predetermined confluence hurtling past exits
but I must salute whomever spared that noble tree
rerouting the fluctuating tide by a few precious feet
within the intricate maze to enable it to sink
tenacious roots into ageless soil and so stand tall
scarred certainly and torn yet undiminished
from generations gone when the westering wagons
sought sanctuary beneath its sheltering boughs
posting a look-out in top-most height
to warn against a dawn attack from the dwindling
tribes who desperate to preserve their native Eden
risked all riding bareback to battle
ululating and war-painted on lean ponies
committed to conserve but prepared to die
alas the lumbering wagons are long gone
so too the thundering herds
but we who straggle behind struggle too
churning our hot rubber over their cold tracks
we are pale imitators of that bygone life
our ghosts are internal and our emotions fragile
as we approach our journey's end
yet we savor secret aspirations
and carry private dreams in our hearts
while we yearn to emulate the great tree's endurance
as it stands serene lifting its proud height to heaven
and reaching beyond today's pollution
that clogs our present
tomorrow's dawn will surely bring another surge
of weary travelers upon this life's congested highway
perhaps another's glance may light
upon the oak's glory and they too may ponder
the sunburst captured in its centered cross
and find peace in its living promise
of what is still to come
beyond the limit of our human sight

Alaska

A land of silent vistas on a vast scale
dominated by heaven's wide arc...
Where rank upon rank of blue-greige mountains
shoulder the skies as far as the eye can see
streaked with pristine glaciers and puddled with snow...
Close beside the road mountain sheep pose picture perfect
defying gravity on dizzying crags
beside torrents of miniature waterfalls
as majestic eagles soar overhead true masters of the sky...
In small scalloped valleys below frail fir trees line the ground
planted in seeming precision resembling
dispirited displaced persons
seeking to be settled someplace else...
Elegant birch groves shade lush tall grasses
edged with hot pink fireweed
and tender tracings of Queen Anne's lace...
Clumps of cheerful daisies and colorful lupines
crowd the banks of wandering streams
all shimmering in the pristine dappled air...
Lakes and inlets lie curiously shallow subject to tidal waves
which on the turn may topple an unwary boat...
Inland swift-flowing clear amber rivers
chart a course beneath emerald spruces
some of them bending low over the water
as though in mock abeyance...
Alas others in their ranks have toppled in
and become mere bleached bones
to shelter the wily salmon
sought by trophy fishermen world-wide
as well as their natural predators
the birds and bears...
It is above all else a land of empty spaces
where the willful wind has obliterated intrepid man's
impermanent imprint
scouring the sere soil clear...
To leave it free to slumber in the half-light
of this tranquil summer night
where the omnipresent sky never quite darkens
and the brooding land bides its time
restless yet unchanged facing this new millennium untroubled
and at peace in a dreamless half sleep...

Thoughts While Roaming Through England and Scotland

Stour Head

Vistas invite as the fast fading light
gilds the smooth bark of some rare tree
too tall to measure
an unseen waterfall at the edge of the lake
draws me on
accompanied by the eerie cries
of a paddling posse of moorhens
I pause beside an ancient urn
and in the uncertain light glimpse a deer
poised amidst dappled shadows
posing like some water sprite
summoned from the deepest depths
shimmering within its smudged shoreline
I long to prolong the image in this secluded glen
but a broken twig breaks the spell
and the elegant fawn bounds from sight
leaving me transfixed
the branches sigh above my head echoing my mood
I shrug and turn away toward a distant light
that beckons me to the comradery in a cozy pub
I hurry away my footsteps hushed
on a carpet of fallen leaves
the sole sound in the lengthening twilight

Birds in a Gilded Cage

While the hedge yet hides them from my eager sight
their chirping songs seize my imagination
filling the freshening air with sweet melody
when finally revealed their perches in filigreed splendor
furnished with exotic vegetation charms
I parade past jostling throngs of children
as curious as myself
but perhaps less aware of the courting rituals
of the vibrant-hued inmates
who flit and float or dart to and fro above the ground
in constantly changing patterns usually in pairs
until I stroll by a solitary jeweled bird
small enough to nestle snug in my palm
he wrenches my heart with his plaintive song
drooping alone on his high perch
placed there perhaps by a disinterested destiny
beside the all-but-invisible mesh of his neighbor's cage
and so a brilliant blue budgerigar
croons in vain to a demure mauve dove
whose docile demeanor denotes submission
to the flawed fate that separates them
don't they know they are different species
from different worlds
perhaps each rejected by their own kind
or are they so beguiled by the beloved's image
that they shun their peers
and savor their isolation from the fluttering crowd below
what unique and stoic resolve do they possess
as they preen and pout only to each other
are they tortured or possibly ignorant
of the bars that segregate them
alas I know not why they like us
should oft-times beat themselves raw
against invisible restraints
when perhaps some pathway might be found
to lead us toward redemption

Lake Windemere

Sheep bleat and swallows swoop
above undulating hills
dipping low to embrace
the gleaming lakes
like some precious infant
held close to a maternal breast
the scent of wild flowers
is snatched by the laughing breeze
from drifts of yellow poppies
and ruby-hued foxgloves
glowing bright against
moss-softened stone walls
a bride in full regalia
blows kisses from the ferry
the lake laps its applause
and I am weightless with joy

Still Life In Beatrix Potter's World

England's Lake District

Imagine a beloved canvas brought to life
the sky a translucent wash of robin's egg blue
abandoned without clouds or showers
when the artists' attention was captivated elsewhere
so nothing mars the azure arc above
or the serene beauty of the lake below
its placid pewter sheen mirrors back to heaven
each luminous blade of marsh grass
and budding water lily home of the humble frog
overhead tree limbs in an infinite variety of green
seem to compete with shaded fern fronds
stilled within the canvas' frame
whilst in the foreground decorous cows pose
in harmonious groups
as creamy lambs nestle beside their ewes
or careen in crazy antics across the grass
all are arranged for best artistic effect
below my window's wide ledge
the neighbor's stone farm
more nearly resembles a child's drawing
perfect in every minute detail
even to the wisp of smoke
curling above a too-tall chimney
a variety of multi-colored blossoms
exquisite with textured brush strokes
tumble in profusion from each almost level surface
be it wall window or white-washed gate post
back lit for special effect two preening doves
strut and coo in coquettish parody on the steep slate roof
a breeze riffles across my face
rippling to life the rosy leaves on the copper beech
edging the close-mown lawn
a swallow flits past my open window
joined in a moment by three or four more
I smile and shake my head in wonder
because this is no painting but my beloved England
laying claim to my recaptured heart

Plockton on the West Coast of Scotland

A single track road
wobbles and weaves
amongst heathers
and foxgloves
and jewel-bright weeds
accompanied by
streams and lochs
and giant tidal seas
bordered by unexpected
very tall palm trees
white-washed cottages
hug the shore
festooned with flowers
which glow forevermore
in the lingering twilight
reflecting back
the pristine clear sea
rimmed by
floating kelp beds
wonderful to see
seals frolic and boat's bob
beneath the castle ruins
that time ere forgot
hand clasps are warm here
and smiles broad
while accents
incomprehensible
convey good will
and bid us welcome
we have stumbled
upon paradise

The Isle of Skye

A limitless land
where views over seas
to the outer Hebrides
-or Heaven itself-
is limited solely by
a humble imagination
a land of convoluted
primordial peaks
and valleys crisscrossed
by frothing tawny waters
few sheep and fewer cattle
graze amongst the occasional
simple stone cottages
standing mute against winter's
promised desolation
and its importuning winds
there is history here
in this time-forgotten remote isle
with its tongue-twister names
where local legends
may be fading into myth
yet memories are generations long
and integrity endures
as ageless as the cliffs
which rim the horizon
standing four-square
and stalwart to defy
the thundering tides
defending this ancient land
from the time before known time
while those who sail her seas
today may seek to capture
her secrets of survival
and simple wisdoms
to aid or console us
in our frenzied yet oft forlorn
brave new modern world

Avebury

The stones command attention
the height at least of two tall men
and broader than a mammoth
they boggle my small mind
How? Who? Where? When?
Why?
The sky above is black
and threatening
until pierced by a rainbow
arcing in unexpected brilliance
above Avebury
our covenant with a benevolent god
pre-dated here by eons of pagan rituals
surely this lush field
is privy to ancient secrets
and sacrifices
when man first sought inspiration
to propagate this fertile land
in the long-lost time
before a jealous god
found us wanting and destroyed all
save a frail few in a fragile ark
repenting
he emblazoned his promise
across the wide sky
proof for all time that man
no more should fear to die
so where do restless spirits go
and by what signs may we know
how to discover those generations
vanished years ago
and essay to clasp hands
and reveal generous hearts
in acceptance of our shared humanity

Cruising To Nantucket

Fog softens pungent air
diffusing light
deadening sound
muffled laughter
bestows
the warmth of friends
life in abeyance
mind weightless
and sleep
serene
peace profound
all around
as resolutions
shaped and grow
sculpt the future
in tempting forms
balancing
expectations
and banishing
anxiety
hope renewed
and love secured
shall my reach
exceed my grasp
safest to drift
amidst
the ebbing tides
temperate embrace
zero visibility
but prospects
unlimited
beckoning from
the further shore

The Bitterroot Ranch on the East Fork of the Wind River in Wyoming

   The sun climbs high in the sky as I dawdle along a rutted
track the river's song my sole company
the scent of sage and pine pungent in the sunshine
the dirt track dimpled by recent rain is spongy underfoot
I pick my way over numerous rocks some striped like zebras
others vivid with burnt-umber lichens
and many more in polished pastel shades of pink
a startling striated turquoise block excites my interest
I lean closer seeking arrowheads but the path beckons me on
my breath grows ragged with the altitude
and showers of golden grasshoppers explode at my feet
whirling away in a clacking cacophony of unwieldy looping
arcs like a child's ill-wound toy I sit on a rock pitted with lichen
and sticky in patches with pine resin a squirrel frisks its tail
chiding me from a cottonwood high overhead
half drowsing in the sun I marvel how this pastoral scene
embraces all my senses
the river is a thing alive coursing its way beside me
a slithering silver ribbon streaming over waterfalls
and swirling in eddies creating miniature whirlpools
or decorously lapping against an occasional smooth sand strand
an angler's paradise where deep shaded pools
harbor wily cutthroat trout
I admire a lone fisherman's dexterity as he casts and casts
again skillfully avoiding overhanging boughs and the bleached
bones of branchless trees spanning the frothing waters
whilst offering a precarious foot-bridge to the further bank
where emerald-green moss mimics a plush carpet
in the dim light
the river's relentless roar crowds out thought
I loll back as high-flying clouds scud above the escarpment
I've become a single simple pin-point of calm in the electric air
where aspen's shimmer above the river's pulsating progress
that carved out this ageless unspoiled Eden
I feast my eyes on the textures and intricate patterns
of some poison-green spores creeping along a fallen pine
whose once-solid trunk was loosened by a flash flood
that swept away all sustaining soil

so now the hapless tree hangs haphazard
above the pounding waters more dead than alive
this winter's burden of snow will surely tumble it down
to join the jumble of giant-sized toothpicks
discarded victims of yesterday's disasters
above the high-tide mark a young tree thrusts out vigorous
new growth from a glacial rock-hewn granite facade
without any visible signs of support
its roots abruptly vanish into the rugged rock
a bush of scarlet currants catches my eye they smear my palm
and are a moist delight in my mouth
I wonder how they escaped the birds and bears
I shake off my lethargy and clamber hand over hand
up the jagged track dislodging boulders
but too fearful to look down until I gain
the brow of the hill where the buffeting wind
snatches away my breath its high-pitched screel
silences the river become invisible now
as it traverses its twisting green-treed tunnel far below
here a new world is revealed to me the horizon rimmed
by distant mountains still sustaining splotches of snow
whilst close by clustering clumps of gray-green sage
cling tenaciously to their exposed roots
and olive-green plateaus in the middle distance
reveal raw scars of red-ocher earth as though all green life
had been ruthlessly stripped away
during the relentless gouging ice age
far beyond mere man's power to control
this scene surely unchanged since men on rough shod ponies
first explored this magical land under the vast sky
at my feet pale plants pincushion the inhospitable soil
as drifts of rosy vetch gentle sharp stones
and patches of purple asters compete with clusters
of yellow daisies stretching away as far as the eye can see
all plants low-grown to escape the scything wind
eyes heavy-lidded in the haze
I visualize bison from an earlier age
thundering up from the dry wash below me
the ground trembling at their snorting approach
I move closer to a single scrub pine to bolster my stance
when a group of riders burst upon the scene
breasting the steep rise they pause beside me
to catch their breath and glory in the grandeur
of this wide-view Wyoming noon time

Benbecula House in the Turks and Caicos

A panoramic seascape envelopes us in beauty
multiple shades of turquoise from the palest
wash of aquamarine
through teal to an unreal
electric blue-green...
Blindingly bright bemuses the senses and slows
the pace of life
to a quiet appreciation brimful
with infinite possibilities...
The chalk white road wends its way
along the slim spine of stark coral
where sisal and cactus stalks
punctuate the gray-green scrub
like exuberant exclamation points
Occasional vivid splashes of bougainvillea
and brilliant orange flamboyant blossoms
enchant...
A handsome house commands superb views
where well-laid terraces and steps lead
to a miniature harbor secreted below
Shifting cloud formations create
dramatic diverse colors
their purple shadows drifting over the
translucent ever-dancing waves...
Whilst in the middle distance
comical islets tease the imagination
resembling long-gone dinosaurs
stretching low to drink

or humped turtles undercut by the restless
choppy sea constantly chipping away coral...
Iridescent-throated hummingbirds
seek nectar as mourning doves coo
seemingly unafraid of the predatory hawks
that hang suspended riding wind currents
as fierce masters of the skies...
The breeze a soothing balm
As scintillating operatic arias
drift through this tropical paradise
accompanied by the sighing wind
and the throbbing base accompaniment
of the ever-surging sea...
We feel ourselves renewed by this
magical place and pause to pay homage
and absorb nature's bounty...
Then blessed and refreshed
and embraced by good friends
we travel on
to seek new adventures
in the wider world...

Escape to Block Island

A long low ripple
warns of a submerged sand bar
as we approach the island's northern tip
under full sail riding the white-flecked waves
in the cobalt blue sea with a blissful abandon
the austere lighthouse resembles a child's primitive
building block toy set down in its treeless landscape
fit for a giant's game of golf with two-toned greens
and immense sand traps scattered about
to challenge their unwieldy skill
the land soon rises to embrace open pastures
and mature trees such as England grows
and I feel at home
'A skillion sticks!' The captain cries
staring at the myriad masts at anchor
glimpsed above the dense bank of wild roses
rimming the Great Salt Pond
we furl our jib and join the procession
where stately yachts and aggressive motor boats
jockey for position
throttled back they throb and growl
at the restraint like scarcely leashed snarling dogs
ready to leap to the attack at a simple touch
we cruise past the averted gaze of cormorants and gulls
who adorn each rock on the breakwater
with lofty disdain
staring seaward with unwavering concentration
as our faint wake laps their solid perch
the beach on our starboard side
is a kaleidoscope of swirling shapes and colors
as laughing kids race in and out of the dancing water
kites fly and frisbees tossed
strangers smile and nod an acknowledgement
of this sublime day
we sail on seeking a secure mooring
alert to the glory of the moment
and fully embracing it

On the Brink Leaving New York City

As we sped away through the gritty
environs of the sprawling city
I saw her for only an instant but our eyes locked
before the car swept us into the tunnel below
her image burned into my mind as a negative
may be imprinted with life by a camera's flash
her gaunt form and shadowed face
imprisoned between clenched hands
scrabbling against a wire cage
resembled some half wild creature gathering strength
before attempting a defiant leap to freedom
or more certain death
her mouth agape mimicked Edvard Munch's 'Scream'
but what of the dusky children clutching her skirts
was she mother or caretaker
would she shepherd them home in the fading light
to torn linoleum under skittering roaches
and scummed syringes discarded in a sink
where discolored sheets lay disordered on a desolate bed
or might her scabbed work weary hands
have their arthritic knuckles bruised by her efforts
to sanitize her corner of an unaware universe
and keep her children richly fed with spiritual values
and even alert to the burning hunger to learn
so that one day they may leave her
and join some future flood of traffic
under this treeless playground
down into the graffiti polluted tunnel below
today become a parody of Christmas past
strewn about with discarded decorations
illumined now by flickering brake lights
a fanciful illusion of Dante's Inferno
or maybe just today's vision of hell
here her young must catch their breath
square their shoulders and essay to look ahead
as they step forth into the promise
of a brightly beckoning new day
intent upon pursuing the illusion
of an abundant life beyond...

Island Paradise in the Dry Tortugas

An cobalt sky arcs above a serene sea
the hazy horizon hard to discern
rimmed by towering cumulus clouds
a putt-putt engine in red rubber dingy
bumps us ashore on the white sand strand
hot sun cool breeze fragrant air
easy to imagine ours the only steps
to imprint this virgin beach
overhead a lazy funnel of frigate birds
conjures up images of pterodactyls
from a bygone age
a splash alerts us to a ponderous turtle
of majestic girth seeking the depths
while exuberant pelicans disjointedly
descend in choreographed precision
to settle on the surface
in the mangrove's cool shade
a solitary skate focuses on an obscure purpose
undulating a shallow hollow
whilst ignoring our enquiring presence
shy horse shoe crabs seek to
camouflage themselves
in the soft as silk sand
and in the uncertain light
hesitant hermit crabs seek refuge
in the pale pearl coral
where miniature star fish abound
alas the ebbing tide signals our return
your hand is warm in mine
as we breast our way forward
on the limpid water's luminous crest
whose smooth glass surface reflects back
the ink-black etching of our sailboat
drifting under the now transformed
blood red sky

The Low Country

Slow paced gray days soft voices and hard lines deep
etched into work-weary dark faces
the unremitting rain soaks the blackened marsh
where few egrets and fewer gulls keep vigil
even the geese have quit the skies and no song bird sings
dispirited boughs hang low displaced by ice
a skeletal hound limps by his eyes bore into mine
I know he's far from home but I cannot help him
an imperial waltz on car radio intimates exile
beneath its lilting tempo it paints pretty pictures
of crinolines sashaying below demure downcast eyes
glowing above alabaster throats clasped in rosy pearls
chaperons' fans flutter in fitful candlelight
casting random reflections over faded silk panels
outdoors camellias and fragrant gardenias stream water
despite the gloom a chandelier pours its splendor
through a three-tiered porch beside a Corinthian Column
a tarnished witness to a more elegant age
our road lies above a rising tide under a lowering sky
I stare absorbed at shrouded windows shielding secrets
yet offering us a rare civility and lodging at twilight
might bygone Belles pace these ancestral halls
in embroidered gowns whispering over worn wood floors
on moon-drenched midnights do they disturb the dreamers
whom heavy-lidded yet may glimpse a candle's pale light
that is soon forgot in the night's slumbering confusion
whilst the ethereal enchantress continually seeks
an elusive repose yet leaves behind tormenting questions
what burdens must she bear that prohibits peace
and why do I sense this nebulous wraith might be my kin
science long-ago labeled 'deja vu' with facile convenience
perhaps in truth we each have walked this way before
today's rain drop mingling with salt tears on my cheek
may tomorrow meld into yonder stream
before pouring itself out into a serpentine river
and so return to the tidal sea from whence we all came
until the sun's heat evaporates it back into atmosphere
where rising on the warm wind's whim it waits
until cooler air condenses it to cloud
whereupon one day a recycled rain drop will fall again
if nature husbands her resources with such maternal love
surely I should never fear for my restless spirit's quest
but trust always that my immortal soul
will be cradled at last in perfect rest

Cruising the Beagle Channel in South America

*Behind us lies the brave Atlantic
whose ferocious wind-tossed cross-currents
join in timeless battle
seeking supremacy over the confluence
of Antarctic current and Pacific ocean
as they collide in gale-force winds
at The Horn
the last inhospitable and least habitable land
on this vast southern continent...
Sailing past in secure splendor
It's hard to imagine the hardships
of the intrepid Dutch navigators who named
this bleak rock at the end of the world
We proceed proudly past mind-numbing fields of glaciers
whose blinding ice-blue beauty births cascades
of frothing torrents to tumble harmlessly beside us
even as their solid bulk shoulders leaden skies
where the solitary albatross dips and glides...
Clouds play an integral part in this poetic drama
billowing forth in stark white shading to gray
or ominous black
till shot through by a shimmering shaft of bright light...
Surely a sign from God Himself
pointing to the perfection of His creation
far removed from mere man's petty pollution
a hopeful foretaste I believe
of His all-encompassing love for us all
that lies beyond the limit of this narrow
earthly sphere
when we each must set brave sail to seek
our ultimate paradise
guided by His divine provenance...*

Venice

A jewel glittering without benefit of sunlight...
The slosh of water against stone
a constant...
At every intersection a bridge
where a multi-national throng pause and
gesture
in thrall to the past but perplexed
how to preserve it...
Clouds hang low lightning strikes
as thunder booms...
In Venice, always, drama reigns!

The Villa Gabriella in Tuscany in Spring

The umber moon is full
slow-rising from the rounded Tuscan Hills
it illuminates ancient stone dwellings
its faint light obscured by fragments
of cloud filaments
yielding intricate designs
among the stark spring vines
planted in serried ranks on myriad terraces
they tumble down from gentle height
the still night is silent
seeming to hold its breath
waiting for the moon's full radiance
to burst free of the cloying wisps of clouds
and stream forth creating stiletto sharp shadows
among the signature pencil-thin cypresses
that point the way along a single stony track
where we pause in homage
to recall the heavy tread of tramping legions
with their foam-flecked chargers
and the slow steps of uncounted simple sandaled folk
who passed this way in eons of other spring times

Sunday Morning in Oregon

The early summer sun streaks its brilliance through tall pines
probing fingers of luminous light to stroke awake
the still-shadowed soft-needled dark
as it brings abundant blessings to the promises
inherent in this bright new day...
Beyond the smooth-planked pale wooden deck
shaded still by breeze-stirred birches
an impressive butterfly bush explodes in giant clusters
of deep magenta it's a magnet
for myriad golden butterflies
who flutter about like exotic insubstantial fans
opening and closing on some primitive whim...
Closer still tri-colored blueberry bushes
offer a moist and flavorful delight
their thin twigs entangled with a fuchsia plant
whose jewel-like blooms succor iridescent hummingbirds...
A solitary deep pink rose brightens the steep slope beyond
would that I could sustain a similar solitary peace
but I carry you beneath my skin inside my heart
so wherever I wander you too are there
and I feel crumpled and incomplete without you...
We sit for a moment in contemplative silence
I study your profile above the bowl of fragrant yellow buds
that we rescued from yesterday's garden pruning labors...
The refreshed restocked fish tank burbles its friendly refrain
and recalls me to the time-fleeting present
where my luggage lies clumped beside it in the hall
awaiting my immediate departure...
I miss you already my heart too full for words
and you've heard them all before
but repetition cannot dilute their simple truth
I love you darling and believe I always will...

Islesboro
A Summer Idyll

The ferry breasts a wake
across mirror smooth water
churning past stands of pine
hugging the rocky shore
as blue mountains
humped like whales
appear hazy on the horizon
glimpses of sandy beaches
in secluded inlets
invokes images of picnic hampers
on bright patterned towels
blessed by the laughter of children
we surge ahead as dolphins' fins
arc away at our approach
and lobster pots weave
and tumble in out wake
osprey's wheel a welcome
in the clear sky above
as we bump ashore
our twisting road
dips past sun-splashed meadows
sprinkled with Queen Anne's lace
and yellow daisies and blue lupines
shimmering in the heat
occasional small shingled cottages
stand in stark simplicity
behind haphazard beds
vibrant with pink and white phlox
everywhere dense foliage
shields the secret pathways
of shy deer
an ageless cemetery
drowses peacefully
in the golden twilight
as we hurry by toward
the warmth of welcome

The Norwegian Dream Crossing the Atlantic

The sapphire sea slips seamlessly by
carrying away all our yesterdays
and conveying us toward
our unknown tomorrows
illuminated by the sun's brilliance
we share hope for a fulfilling future
overflowing with multi-faceted gifts
as time and tides flow serenely past
we're lulled into accepting
past regrets and focus instead
on the boundless horizon's
bountiful promise
beside my deck chair
a tropical bird with luminous plumage
beats the air with measured strokes
I pray she'll stay for a moment's respite
but she falls behind our churning wake
I mourn her passing as I stand alone
mulling myriad questions
where did she come from
and where does she go
our days are brimful with play
and each night offers
glittering amusements
yet I pause before sleep
to absorb the ocean's undulating embrace
that draws to the surface long ago
mislaid memories of childhood
I stand alone late at night
Staring transfixed through
the cabin window
watching white spume flying past
like the mane on a galloping horse
in molten movement
swallowed by the insatiable sea
that spawned all known life
depthless and unchanging
from time everlasting
and vibrantly alive tonight
under the starless sky...

Reflection

Reflection

1. 911 206
2. Family Wedding 209
3. The Beach in Autumn 210
4. Diana Princess of Wales 213
5. Nostalgia: Is Youth Wasted on the Young 217
6. Saying Good-bye 218
7. Third Rate Artists 221
8. Sandi the Spaniel 222
9. Reunion in Suffolk 225
10. A Radiant Life 226
11. Windows in My Mind 229
12. After He's Gone 230
13. How Could I Bid Love Good-bye 233
14. Remembering Mars My Retired Racehorse 234
15. A Walk in the Woods 237

911

Shock disbelief dismay
the unthinkable happening here to us
the most generous nation the world has ever known...
Beautiful buildings and the inviolate center of our security
implode as desperate men leap
to lose their lives...
Like a slow-motion movie
that we do not want our children to see
but this is real life not reel life evil
and it replays and replays in all its graphic
grueling gruesome enormity
in hundreds of comfortable homes on wide-screened TV...
We ask the unanswerable 'Who did this?'
'Why do they hate us?'
'What have we done or not done to them?'
Overwhelmed sickened satiated we turn away in pain...
But slowly and surely our panic and paralysis turn to pride in
whom we are...
Diverse different-cultured people bonded now as never before
in common cause...
So we stand strong shoulder to shoulder
as grace and resilience and resolve
surge back to fill us with rare courage
and a profound pride in whom we are
and all that we may yet be...
Well-loved well-remembered words of homage
to our nation
catch in our throats clogged now with simple emotion
as we unite to applaud and honor our elected leaders
in our blessedly free and democratic country...
Our eyes brim in witness to gestures of kindness
amongst strangers
and the brave acts of selfless heroism
from millions more still unknown...
...And some say turn the other cheek watch and pray...
As our military readies to retaliate without delay...
So we struggle to find a balance
and return to routine work school and even play...
As we mourn our lost way of life and loved-ones known
and thousands more lying in unmarked
but never-to-be-forgotten mass graves

on a day that has changed all of us forever...
So we hug in unspeakable sorrow and hope to stifle
the stabs of anxiety that pierce our souls
as we question child-like
'Can this evil return? Where? When?
And who next may be asked to pay the ultimate price?
And who amongst us may yet be spared?'
We need rather to heed the still small voice within
as we pray for resolution patience and above all peace
in our world gone wrong...
That a light may be lit within each one of us
to purge our faults
and shine bright purpose upon the uphill way ahead
so that the whole world may soon follow our lead
and forgive one another but see justice done
and give back to humanity the best
that we each have within us to give...
So we stride ahead with quiet fortitude
to embrace the future
and set our feet with new-found strength of purpose
upon the true path ahead
essaying to right the wrongs
even as we hope to heal our wonderful
but sorely wounded world...

Family Wedding

I awaken at still of night
and without turning on a light
open my memory book
stirring leaves from trees long gone
seeking faces I cannot easily find
whilst searching the secret
corners of my mind
I touch my own face
as if there I could know
and find the wisdom to halt
emotions that flow so fast
conveying by their expression
experiences long past
I wish my thoughts to be fair
to balance the darker penance I bear
essaying too late now to right wrongs
or undo scarcely scabbed-over harms
yet we're all needful of redemption here
and must accept soothing balms
why then my head still restless on my pillow
while tears trickle down
like leaves drift from a willow
shedding its reflection into opaque pool
whose stagnant surface reflects back
simply the image of a fool
for a glass alas mirrors only what is done
no one can yet see what is still to come
and none of us here can rewrite the past
so we must accept all and close the book at last
loving ourselves and forgiving our sins of omission
while we face the abyss
of frequent faults of commission
and strive hard to gentle the sharp edges of regret
and hopefully succeed to protect
all that once was good
so we treasure the gifts God freely gave in the past
and hand on the torch to those beloved and forgiven
sending them forth now in peace to move unbidden
into the warmth of the sun's embrace
and face with courage the dawn
of this their new day

The Beach in Autumn

The sun is bright dazzling despite my glasses
so I squint as I swing my arms
and stride along the low tide's
object-strewn fluctuating line
seeking treasures from the sea and inhaling iodine
from discarded heaps of discolored seaweed...
Gulls grumble at my approach
and hop stiff-legged a few token yards away
before lifting into brief flight
and settling behind me onto hard-ribbed sand
the sand almost motionless
reflects glass-shards of brilliant light
and the pattern of clouds overhead makes me smile
in remembrance of the child I once was who dreamed dreams
creating castles from fanciful shapes
always eager to explore far away places
whenever a tall sail silhouetted on the horizon beckoned...
I climb wind-weathered stairs past rows of empty cabanas
to discover a discarded purple ribbon
tangled in a skein of seaweed I pause to wonder...
Did some summer breeze tease it free
from a tow headed child's un-bleached pony tail
or was it a gay decoration pinned to a daring décolletage
below coquettish smile and heavy-lidded glance
as violins shimmered melody under the striped tents
and couples swayed close beneath the moon's potent gaze
whilst lazy waves murmured their approval...
Where is it's owner now hunched over school books
As the summer's tan fades faint freckles from her face
Or is some lithe long-limbed beauty
Skipping cracks on city streets
Whilst dreaming of chalets for Christmas...
I love this place and season best
When I am the sole beachcomber here
Free to meditate or create fantasies
Whilst shorter days yet provide warmth
Where I sprawl against a barred beach door
Relishing the day and feeling blessed in the moment
And so grateful for so much in my life...

Diana Princess Of Wales

We look beyond the glittering facade
of lean fit healthy body
beautiful face and swept-back hair
above unforgettable clear blue eyes
to her compassionate heart
that showed a small nation and a big world
how to love

How also to honor the often despised
diseased and displaced ones
whom few called friend
central to her life was her role as mother
protector advisor and fun-filled adventurer
quick to embrace or soothe hurts
and able to lighten unimaginable burdens with laughter

Her experiences and emotions
were larger than ours
emblazoned in headlines around the world
and few private moments remained inviolate
yet she survived most things
to emerge intact and even radiant
projecting a beacon of hope to the disadvantaged

Many believed she was a bright promise
for a future gentled by tolerance
a fable for our times emulated by women
at opposite and often opposing
ends of the spectrum
whether society matrons
indulging their quest for the latest fashion fads

Or serious seekers of truth searching
for a way to prohibit crippling landmines
and end the isolation that ignorance brings to illness
she gave encouragement to so many who endure so much
diminished by poverty and hunger
surviving lives stripped of possibilities
here too she led the way

And shone a light into their sun-starved shadows
that polite society eschews
she focused world attention
on human problems that most people prefer to disregard
perhaps now we may take courage
from her hands-on approach to charity
would that we could also emulate her empathy

*Now alas she's gone
snatched from us
in the first flush of maturity
taking tentative steps toward personal happiness
while unflagging in her perceived duties
as a public persona of whom much was demanded
and to whom no quarter was given*

*The shy Di grown into the most famous
woman in the world
the private Di a model for motherhood
her unique gift for humanity
brought her a world of admirers
while her insecurities allowed her to be hurt
by the carping criticisms of some of her peers*

*Her absence from the world's stage devastates
we'll always remember where we were
when we heard the news...
our sympathy for her sons is as boundless
as our respect for her
brave Princess may God grant you His peace
and allow your example to remain in our hearts
as an inspiration to love and serve others*

Nostalgia: Is Youth Wasted on the Young

Maturity is compromise:
A suppression of instinctual feelings
until they wither and die.
Cerebral intellect triumphs over dwindling emotions
as words thwart actions.
But then who wins? How rekindle an ardor
that lingers still in the base of the brain
when nerves have been ordered not to comply?
Constricted by logic we dutiful sheep blindly follow the herd
our fling flung and intoxicating ecstasies
buried under the weight of day to day moralizations.
We emerge – adult! Reasonable! Hypocritical shams.
Mere husks of all that we were born to be.
The world no longer well lost for love
we serve those others within our narrow sphere
of responsibility.
And applaud ourselves for our civic minded
generosity displayed amongst the trappings of success.
In the world's eyes we prosper
while in secret we strive to suppress the shriveling whisper
that our spirit is suffocating.
And I let you do this to me! I engaged in my soul's death
squeezing myself back into the conforming mold.
Doing what others do. Behaving as society dictates
and the world condones.
Ah! Sweeter shores of love!
Where once our dreams birthed hope
in my depths of hurt there yet hides the faltering light
of a still-watchful still waiting child
wishing for the mystical reunion with it's other half.
Wait in vain. All is lost. Mind over matter! Fact before fiction!
Reality of compromise over the delusion of perfection.
Life is not fair and we are flawed creatures indeed
So I must permit my interior life to leave.
Allow the daily grind to wear away
the pitted surface of the promise of love
as knife sharp reality cuts deep into my soul
bleeding out all tender tendrils of hope
until death itself will come
and I pray then that the ghosts of paradise lost
will fade away as surely as a perfect peace is promised...

Saying Goodbye

Each life contains
An inborn light
A radiance residing
deep within us
A gift that never withers
And cannot die
Yet ebbs and flows
And rarely shows
Its brilliance
But to be fully human
Is to be touched
By the divine
And some among us are
Exceptional souls
Who sorely tested
Yet remain true
And humble us
By their example
Of walking
With steadfast hope
And resolute courage
Through the valley
Of the shadow of death
Assured that
In an instant
They will be transformed
To emerge
Into everlasting life
Accepting the sacred
Promise
Given to all
Who live by faith
That in due season
We will be restored
By Heaven
And gathered
In peace
Into the outstretched arms
Of our ever - loving God

Third Rate Artists

*The freezing wind penetrates my skin with icy shards
pricking a trickle of tears onto my frozen cheeks
I enter the warm studio with relief but step back in dismay
wishing the wind had entered with me
to whisk away the heaps of jumbled canvasses
crowded with obscure mud-colored forms...
The artists' distorted perceptions seems perchance
to mimic their disordered lives
as devoid of obvious talent they exist precariously
amidst this damaged disarray
surrounding themselves with clumsy chaos
whilst a creeping inertia evaporates their scant gifts
and self-delusional illusions
that one day they may yet produce something of value...
Poor valiant souls their fraudulent and fractured vision fails
for want of simple inspiration
yet they refuse to bow to lessons unlearned
and turn blindly aside from past abortive possibilities
amidst the ruin of lost potential
and the annihilation of their dreams...
They stubbornly essay to forge a new path
beyond the flood-tide of current prestige and popularity
showered upon the fortunate few
so they slop ever more paint onto ever more canvasses
hoping to be overtaken by a flash flood of inspiration
to sweep them into the realm of public acclaim...
Can any one of us in fact do more
perhaps we too are bound by our own inarticulate hopes
lying stillborn in our yearning soul's secret recesses
should we not applaud and even encourage
their dogged pursuit of skewered images...
I turn away and tug open the heavy door
relieved to be released into the fresh air
shivering I walk away
wondering what inner turmoil
conspires to hold these artists captive
to create such endless empty vistas
from their meager imaginations
even as I applaud their efforts
because one day lightening may indeed strike
and it must take supreme courage
to exhibit your dreams
and risk the censor of your peers...*

Sandi the Spaniel

Soulful brown eyes
a beautifully proportioned compact body
inside lustrous fur of softest silk
sporting distinctive black and white markings...
Legs on springs!
Enable her to leap like a gazelle
and pirouette like a circus star
and steal edible treats from impossible places...
A beguiling personality
her stub of a tail
quivers her whole body
into a wriggling welcome
whenever her mistress comes home...
Unquestioned loyalty
she would defend her own
against any and all imagined threats
but personally she prefers
the passive approach...
Her head on your shoe as she sprawls
her hind legs stretched out flat
she lies limp with bliss
or bats her big eyes to advantage
begging for a pat
before she rolls over and
exposes her tummy
to be tickled...
She seeks the best
in each of us
would that we could
share her blessedly uncomplicated
and simplistic world
and her completely devoted
dogged view of life...

Reunion in Suffolk

Has it really been 20 years since we last laughed together?
the time bridged by 'sound bite' notes
hurried 'head line' phone calls
and most often pages and pages of unruly writing
as husbands were lost - and found -
and children's knife-sharp problems endured...
These thoughts like photographs
glimpsed through fast moving pages
flit though my mind
as the train makes rhythmic progression north
toward the eastern coastline that I once knew and loved
I sway in my seat and my heartbeats accelerate
in keen anticipation as England's pastoral beauty
flows past the wide windows soothing my soul
and filling me with the certainty
that this sacred land is indeed my spirit's home
the pace lessens and a quick glimpse as I step down
brings unexpected tears
we embrace and I am bereft of speech as my throat clogs
but not for long!
Soon we are engaged in a stream-of-consciousness
reminiscing, reminding and reliving
those golden days of sun and fun
when we explored the world extending our own horizons
and anything was possible because we were young...
Other memories stab the heart
too intimate to share with a stranger
but comforting beyond psychiatry to have
your compassion because you were there
and saw the hard choices to be made...
Sharing past regrets purges the pain
our bond has withstood time we are closer than siblings
and soon feel liberated and reinvigorated
rather than resigned
to face the future with quiet confidence
born from the realization that we have survived much
and gained insights and wisdom
that will enable us to explore the days that lie ahead
with an unflagging sense of humor
and an insatiable curiosity for what comes next

A Radiant Life

Her life is hanging by a thread
But her eyes sparkle with joy each day
and her zest for life is contagious
the reality of her world encompasses too much
to be captured in mere words
medical protocols are administered with precision
like a regimented army offering salvation
with one miracle drug at a time
hands on holistic healing
is evident as well
but far more than either of these
she is surrounded by love
love of husband of children
and the unmeasured devotion
from life-long cherished friends
and even casual acquaintances
who sense something unique within her
a generosity of spirit that embraces us all
abundant courage and grace under pressure
a rare acceptance of what will be
the only certainty
for the legions who love and hope
is that we who witness her battle
are convinced of her ultimate triumph
and we are all changed
by sharing the gift of her journey
as she shines a bright light on her path ahead
while her indomitable, indelible presence
will live within us forever
offering each one of us comfort
as long as our lives shall last
and beyond...

Windows In My Mind

I no longer can find
the path to your heart-
the precious part
of what was once so real...
Now turned to dust
and blown away
full grown dismay
faint echoes fond remembrance
bearing a resemblance
yet disintegrating disinterest
fails again the crying test
collapsing in the bitter sound
of lives no longer tightly bound
the close-knit harmony we played
long since frayed...
All trust betrayed...
Gnawing sorrow of hope all slayed
intensity prolonged
but could not sustain
the searing truth
that passion's precipice
ends in choking blackness
and a mind turned inward
cannot look forward
"Come, take my hand,
and we'll build castles
in the sand..."
But the tides of time
no longer turn for you...
Morning missed the lips
I'd kissed
in night-time bliss
now mourning mist obscures
all expectations
casting shadows 'cross the
memories from the windows
in my mind...

After He's Gone

*This is the sound of his absence
silence
this is the size of the hurt
immense
an indentation on a pillow
shadows a ghostly remembrance
his scent is carelessly laundered away*

*Each day's grief an accumulated
burden
I am hollow fragmented weary
does anyone care
my mind plays tricks
leaping sequences to illuminate
memories lost*

*Birdsong trills me awake each
dawn
flowers frame my window
roses redolent of summer
fragile receptacles of dew
swallows swoop
above new-mown hay*

*The breeze ruffles hair from my
face
drying salt tears from my cheeks
beauty and solitude
embrace my senses while
the utter peace
splinters my soul*

How Could I Bid Love Good-Bye

How should I erase you from my heart?
How might I obliterate the trace of your fingers
from my fevered skin?
How train my brain not to remember the gift
of your murmured endearments
and the intent cobalt gaze that precedes touch...
Who invited love in?
It was suddenly there in the electric air
full-blown and seemingly by whim
a tiny seed caught in my heart
nurtured by kindness and respect ...
It warmed me through
and flowered into full-blown welcome
transforming mundane days
into incandescent explosions of bliss
overlaid by lilting laughter
that transformed the very ordinary
by some lover's alchemy into the
so extraordinary...
The morning birdsong finds an echo within my heart
and popular songs strike a responding chord there too.
How did I ever dare to face life alone?
Now that you share my vision
past regrets stay past and previous mistakes forgiven
even the future holds no fear...
I am content to live fully and love totally
in the present
wishing only to share whatever comes
with you...

Remembering Mars: My Retired Racehorse

Hoofbeats In The Night

A quick tattoo
A sudden volley of sound
Of crunching gravel kicked against my window
And then the fading rhythm of diminishing hoof beats
Da-dum, da-dum, da-dum...
I stir uneasily am I awake and this is real?
Or sleeping and nightmare haunted?
Either way Mars has gone to greener pastures...
Does anyone else toss restless in remembrance
On their pillow?
Does anyone else's heart pound in sympathy?
Mars had beauty and speed, truly a noble beast
With a brave heart and glossy black coat
With a distinctive V of white
Striking against his dense blackness
On the top of his tail...
How he loved to gallop gobbling up the ground
Sweat making the reins slippery in my hands
He possessed a keen intelligence
And a willingness to learn to jump
Always a pleasure to groom
Nuzzling me as I moved around him
He would nicker a welcome whenever I entered his stall
And neigh a resonating hello and race over to the fence
Each time I approached him grazing in the paddock...
Does he lie soundly now in a heavenly bed
Piled high with fragrant straw?
Or does his joyful spirit
Lead him to race the shadows of moonlight
Dancing across the elysian fields?
Does he remember his impatience as
I placed my foot in his stirrup
And he accepted my eager weight upon his back
As we flew together toward the uncharted stars?
What happy fantasies for a frosty night!
Would that my eventual peace could reunite us...

A Walk in the Woods
(a childhood memory)

A fragment of a recurring dream from childhood...
My world is turned topsy-turvy...
America
a land of bright light and familiar routine
has receded like a miniature precise view
glimpsed through the lens of a telescope...
Survived was the sea-sick trip back to England
with the ship's pool full of potatoes...
Now even the sun has abandoned me here
as each dirge gray day drags past...
I am without my siblings homeless displaced
averting my eyes from too-recent bomb craters
whilst striving to ignore the deprivations
that make my empty stomach clench...
And far too frightened at age nine to look ahead
or attempt to process the past
that led me to this achingly cold place...
My single friend a black lab
whose impure puppies
were ripped from her and drowned at birth
much as I might have wished to be...
My loneliness is palpable
I curl up for part of each day
in her rough wooden doghouse
relishing her warmth and friendship
free from prying eyes
in a disused corner of the vast stable yard...
This late afternoon I follow
my four legged friend's whimpered insistence
away to the woods...
Out of sight of the imposing house
situated on its impressive estate
of manicured lawns and regimented flower beds
her head lifts her tail wags
and she pauses often to reassure herself
that I am following along the rutted track...
The trees so close-planted here
It's hard to glimpse the dull pewter sky

*A holly tree vivid with scarlet berries
reveals another friend
a bright eyed robin small enough
to fit snug in my child's palm...
The silence is absolute
until I crunch through patches of dead leaves
filigreed with frost...
I step with care around their brittle edges
until something gives me pause
and I look up awestruck
at the immensity of this haven...
And a warm feeling steals over me
as if I am to play an integral part
in some reverent event
to be celebrated in this natural nave...
I draw in a deep breath
pungent with mold and distant wood-smoke
and stand in hushed homage
with my arms wide spread...
I close my eyes and I'm flooded by the feeling
that I have found sanctuary here
nurtured by nature and therefore at peace
in this secluded earthly paradise...
I have been sorely tested in the years since
surviving even the unthinkable
death of a beloved son...
But this profound peace
encountered for the first time
in the depths of the woods embrace
during some desperate days of childhood...
Has stayed with me ever since
to lighten the burdens sufficient unto each day
and shine clear light upon my way
as I forge ahead with quiet resolution
to keep promises as fragile as a discarded leaf...
So that I may continue my pilgrimage
hoping to explore and expand
and even to relish the new experiences
I may encounter in my not yet completed life...*

www.ingramcontent.com/pod-product-compliance
Lightning Source LLC
Chambersburg PA
CBHW041801290426
43661CB00132B/1267